Lakeland

PICTURING CHANGE

RANDALL M. MACDONALD,
SUSAN PRIEST MACDONALD & SARAH E. MACDONALD

THE History PRESS

Published by The History Press
Charleston, SC 29403
www.historypress.net

First published 2009

Manufactured in the United States

ISBN 978.1.59629.702.9

Library of Congress Cataloging-in-Publication Data

MacDonald, Randall M., 1961-
Lakeland : picturing change / Randall M. MacDonald, Susan Priest MacDonald, and
Sarah E. MacDonald.
p. cm.
Includes bibliographical references.
ISBN 978-1-59629-702-9
1. Lakeland (Fla.)--Pictorial works. 2. Lakeland (Fla.)--History--Pictorial works.
3. Lakeland (Fla.)--Buildings, structures, etc.--Pictorial works. 4. Historic buildings-
-Florida--Lakeland--Pictorial works. I. MacDonald, Susan Priest, 1958- II.
MacDonald, Sarah E. III. Title.
F319.L22.M337 2009
975.9'67--dc22
2009039527

To Malcolm Murdoch MacDonald and Constance Marsh MacDonald,
who model the beauty of inquiry.

Contents

Foreword

After the personally rewarding experience of restoring a 1914 farmhouse for our family's home in the mid-1970s, I became interested in historic preservation and attended a workshop at Largo's Heritage Park. Dwight Young, then the Southeast director of the National Trust for Historic Preservation, made a statement I have quoted often: "Future generations will judge us by what we build and by what we tear down." Downtown Lakeland was launching an effort to compile a master plan, and I feared Lakeland was about to lose more of the familiar fabric that was still left in downtown.

I was pleasantly surprised when I met Jim Edwards and learned that he and Wayne Dewhirst were working on completing Florida Master Site File forms on each of the downtown buildings. A native Lakelander with a passion for his city, Jim encouraged me to organize a group that would advocate for historic preservation. Mildred Grizzard and I founded Historic Lakeland, Inc., in September 1979 and immediately began to call attention to the sadly neglected Lake Mirror Promenade. Historic Lakeland encouraged the city to consider enacting a preservation ordinance. Fortunately, the new city attorney was David Cardwell, who had studied at the University of Florida School of Law under Dr. Roy Hunt, one of the founders of the Florida Trust for Historic Preservation. The preservation ordinance Cardwell authored in 1981 has served Lakeland well, protecting Lakeland's few remaining landmark buildings from demolition or drastic modifications.

I believe Lakeland now has a preservation ethic—a community conscience that asks questions such as "Do we really want to give up that important element of Lakeland's skyline?" and "Are we certain that we want to sacrifice the parklike setting surrounding the Park Trammell Building?" Don't we wish these kinds of questions had been asked before we lost the beautiful Hotel Thelma or the whole block of retail shops on the south side of Main Street between Florida and Tennessee Avenues?

This amazing collection of pictures depicting scenes from Lakeland's past and comparing what exists there today serves as a dramatic reminder of the richness of our town's fabric, much of it sadly torn away. I commend the authors and hope that this work will encourage future generations to cherish our community's uniqueness.

Jean Bunch
Co-founder, Historic Lakeland, Inc.

Acknowledgements

A relaxing rainy day lunch conversation in the Kentucky Building provided the impetus for this volume. We wondered how many diners knew that this building once had the town's most distinctive façade, who would remember the Magic Fountain in Munn Park and which of our friends made their first big furniture purchase from Kirk McKay? How many remember the sharp whistle from the Lake Mirror power plant marking midday or boarded their first train at Munn Park? Who spent their first night in town at the Hotel Thelma?

A walking tour of downtown reveals hints of Lakeland's past, from its initial development as a retail and residential center to the effects of mid-century sprawl to a gradual, purposeful revitalization of the city's center. We wished to chronicle those changes, and to the extent that we have been successful, we owe a great deal to the generosity of others.

This project would not have been possible without the steadfast and cheerful assistance of Kevin Logan and Ruth Snyder of the Lakeland Public Library Special Collections Department. Their knowledge of Lakeland's people, places and events is wide-ranging, and they generously shared material critical to the project. Others who provided assistance include Jean Bunch; Kayla Lipham and Nicholas McDowell of the Terrace Hotel; Nell Thrift of the Florida United Methodist Conference Archives; Barbara Myers and James Bronkhorst at Reececliff; and Colby and Cissy Brown. The History Press has been wonderful to work with, from our initial conversations with Allison Stauble to the guidance of Laura All, Julie Scofield and Ryan Finn.

We also appreciate the support and encouragement of Kay Anderson, Cindy Anthony, Joy Banks, Audrey Bebensee, Rachel A. Bomberger, Carol Acorn Busby, Debbie Carmack, Sandy Danna, Mike Denham, Alex Falcone, Mary M. Flekke, Nora Galbraith, Anne B. Kerr, Diana Koehler, Lisa Lapointe, LuAnn Mims, Krystal Newman, Kaye Smith Newton, Brittney Piescik, Ann Rogers, James G. Rogers Jr., Debbie Rusch, Eridan J. Thompson, Stephen Tucker, Grethe Ullrich, Justin Vergara, Russell G. Warren, SaraLou Wilkerson and Marsha Yoder. Special appreciation goes to Betty Jo Priest and to Constance Marsh MacDonald and Malcolm M. MacDonald.

Lakeland holds a special place for us, just as it does for so many others, and we look forward to seeing what comes next as the unending history of Lakeland unfolds.

Introduction

Herbert Drane liked what he saw. The twenty-year-old engineer was supervising construction of Henry B. Plant's railroad line through a remote, wooded, central Florida area dotted with lakes in June 1883. He established a camp on Lake Wire before moving on with the railroad but returned in November to settle at this highest point along the mainline between Tampa and Jacksonville. Drane was not the first to settle here—Jesse Keen, J.W. Futch and their families were ensconced west of Lake Wire, Archie McLeod had planted orange groves long ago on the north shore of Lake Hollingsworth where Native Americans lived centuries before and other homesteads were located near unspoiled lakes. But Drane arrived at a particularly opportune time, as the railroad opened this new frontier to land prospectors and other adventurous types who braved uncertain conditions to create the beginnings of a modern town out of the forested wilderness.

Joining Drane were others who saw promise here—eighty acres north of the railroad were purchased and platted by Reuben C. Clough and brothers L. Luther Trammell, Erasmus R. Trammell and John W. Trammell during November and December 1883. Clough and the Trammells sold their first lots in December 1883 and January 1884. From Kentucky came Abraham Godwin Munn, who arrived in February 1884 and purchased eighty acres south of the Clough and Trammell property and another several thousand acres in the vicinity. Munn, Samuel A. Hartwell and Charles W. Hillman organized the Lakeland Improvement Company for the purpose of promoting settlement and constructed the Tremont House (later Hotel) overlooking Lake Mirror in 1885.

Munn won early influence when his offer to build a railroad station at his own expense was accepted by the railroad, and his $2,500 station helped establish the center of town. Munn donated land for a city park south of the depot, and although he never lived here permanently, he is considered the city's founder. Lakeland was incorporated by thirty-four voters on January 1, 1885, at which time the city's name was selected. The city limits included four square miles.

William B. Bonacker purchased a lot from Munn to establish the city's first store at the present site of Nathan's Men's Store, and D.H. Slone Sr. constructed another in the present-day Bowyer Block, home of Brooke Pottery. L.J. Nieuwenkamp's bank was established in 1886, and electricity arrived in 1891. The city continued to attract residents, and by 1893 twenty trains passed through Lakeland daily. Churches were organized, the school thrived, agricultural commodities were developed and in 1902 the city gained a sense of permanence when handsome brick buildings began to replace frame structures. Over the next decade, the population increased from one thousand to eight thousand residents, and Lakeland thrived during the Florida land boom.

The late 1920s were particularly challenging, as Lakeland felt the effects of the land bust and the Depression. The city felt a sense of renewal in the 1930s and 1940s, beginning when the Detroit Tigers arrived to hold spring training in Lakeland in 1934. Lakeland's Food Machinery Corporation manufactured amphibious Water Buffalo personnel carriers during World War II. By the 1950s, Lakeland had become a bustling city of 30,851, with industry, schools, hospitals, an airport and other conveniences of a modern city. Florida Southern College was attracting thousands of visitors to the world's largest single-site collection of Frank Lloyd Wright architecture. All the while, downtown Lakeland reflected the evolving needs of its citizens. Buildings came and went, and unfortunately, some of those lost held a character that their replacements did not possess.

What became of young Herbert Drane? He established an insurance company in 1887, helped build the Kentucky Building in 1903 and built the Drane Building on East Main Street. He was Lakeland's fifth mayor, a county commissioner, a member of the Florida House of Representatives and Senate and served in the U.S. House of Representatives from 1917 to 1933. Perhaps this was to be expected from one of the city's visionaries.

The purpose of this volume is to illustrate changes that have occurred to buildings in and near downtown, using historic images paired with photographs from 2009. We hope you enjoy this glimpse of Lakeland's history and are inspired to support efforts to preserve its historic character for future generations.

Munn Park

DOWNTOWN OASIS

Downtown Lakeland: Rich Traditions…Artful Energy." More than just a marketing catchphrase, this slogan pays homage to the authentically historic nature of Munn Park and the surrounding area. Munn Park provides a sense of focus for a vibrant downtown, where public art and gardens promote creativity and enhance the quality of life. Abraham G. Munn donated the public gathering space to the community that in 1908 was renamed Munn Park in his honor. The modern park is bordered on three sides by restaurants, commercial firms, retail establishments and public agencies.

The first train passed through Lakeland on the way from Kissimmee to Tampa in 1884, and the Cedar Street parking lot now stands where a succession of railroad stations delivered passengers to Lakeland's grand hotels. Munn's two-story station was replaced by a single-story wooden station, which in turn gave way to a brick station in 1912. Although a devastating 1918 fire destroyed the core of the station, it was rebuilt with an additional floor and incorporated the original brick walls. It is difficult to overstate the importance of the railroad and related industries to the historic development of Lakeland. The city existed because of the railroad, and in 1922 the railroad payroll was the chief source of local income, amounting to nearly $100,000 per month. The population of Lakeland was 10,587, and 500 worked for the railroad.

The grounds of Munn Park have evolved as public tastes changed. One constant since 1910 has been the monument to Confederate dead erected by the United Daughters of the Confederacy. Dedication of the monument coincided with creation of walking paths that transformed the green space into a more formal garden. The park hosted concerts and other public events, including an appearance by Theodore Roosevelt, who in 1917 addressed Lakelanders at the Atlantic Coast Line Railroad station regarding the world war. Images from the 1920s and 1930s show the park's elevated bandstand, which housed the city's records until goats broke in and consumed important papers.

Angular walkways, benches, small pavilions and a large lighted, musical "Magic Fountain" were installed in 1961. Aerial views of Munn Park in the mid-1960s show a rather bleak space with few remarkable trees. By the late 1960s, downtown was losing stores to Southgate Shopping Center, Searstown and other suburban malls. The revitalization of Munn Park was central to bringing merchants and shoppers back downtown, and that effort began in earnest in the late 1980s. The park was recreated as a lightly wooded public gathering space with wide brick walkways—including 1,900 personalized bricks—reminiscent of its appearance in the 1910s. The walkway and a decorative fountain were dedicated in 1993.

The Munn Park Historic District was created in 1980 and certified in 1983, and it was listed on the National Register of Historic Places in 1997. The district recognizes the oldest commercial structures in the city and the importance of the city's first public space. The city has many other attractive parks, but none is as connected to the earliest history of Lakeland.

The photographs in this chapter show the buildings surrounding Munn Park. The arrangement is clockwise beginning near the southeast corner of the park, where East Main Street meets South Kentucky Avenue.

Some six thousand U.S. soldiers from New York, Ohio and Massachusetts encamped in Lakeland before departing for Tampa and Cuba at the onset of the Spanish-American War in 1898. On the east and north shores of Lake Wire from May 16 to June 7 were First Lieutenant John J. Pershing and his storied Tenth Cavalry. This photograph depicts five soldiers during drills on East Main Street near the corner of Kentucky Avenue, facing the city park. *Courtesy Special Collections, Lakeland Public Library.*

Columbus W. Deen (1861–1927) and Robert Bryant (1849–1925) constructed the Deen-Bryant Building for $13,522 in about 1912 at 221 East Main Street. Home in the 1940s to Liggett's Rexall drugstore and McCrory's, it is now the landmark Nathan's Men's Store established by Nathan and Mildred Estroff. The adjacent Elliston Building (circa 1912) housed Charles I. Dwiggins's Central State Bank, founded in 1920, and later the Darling Shop from about 1934 until 1965. The store's name remains at the old entranceway. *Authors' collection.*

Abraham G. Munn's Lakeland Building and Improvement Company constructed the town's first masonry building south of the railroad. The Kentucky Building (1903) located at 205–209 East Main Street was also architect Wilbur B. Talley's first local structure. Physician William Rowan Groover and dentist Willis S. Irvin both had offices here. This circa 1908 photograph depicts a weathered two-story wood-frame real estate and insurance office building to the east, illustrating Lakeland's transition toward substantial, "permanent" structures. *Courtesy Special Collections, Lakeland Public Library.*

Postmaster Joseph L. Skipper erected the three-story brick building at 211–217 East Main Street that today bears his name. After the post office relocated to South Tennessee Avenue, the Skipper Building (1912) housed the Lerner Shops clothing boutique and other establishments and, following a 2000 restoration, now provides office space for MidAmerica Administrative and Retirement Solutions. Tommy Elliott's Linksters Tap Room at 209 East Main includes exterior seating flanked by flat-screen televisions—quite a change compared to one hundred years earlier! *Authors' collection.*

This 1910–11 image depicts the Kentucky Building and a furniture store south of Munn Park. Erving G. Tweedell's grocery and meat market was located at 205 East Main Street. Other structures along East Main include Norman Riggins's store at the southwest corner with South Tennessee Avenue. The Kentucky Building's central second-floor balcony was enclosed and the elaborate brick and masonry arched façade was altered, both in the 1940s. *Courtesy Special Collections, Lakeland Public Library.*

The interior of Black and Brew Coffee House and Bistro at 205 East Main Street offers a glimpse at the original magnificence of the Kentucky Building. Owners Chris and Mike McArthur oversaw a transformation that revealed many of the building's original features prior to the February 2006 opening. Once a lively shopping area, all of the buildings in the 100 block of East Main Street have been demolished in recent decades. *Authors' collection.*

Moore's Style Shop at 207 East Main Street predominates this 1924 Earl Morgan Savage photograph. Other occupants of the Kentucky Building included the Lake Pharmacy drugstore, dentist Willis S. Irvin, physician Benjamin Maynard and realtor Oliver Schoonover. To the east were Cyrus and Frances Wolfson's Famous Department Store in the Skipper Building, Central State Bank, City Drug Store and, past South Kentucky Avenue, First National Bank. Construction scaffolding is visible at the Terrace Hotel, which opened in October 1924. *Courtesy Special Collections, Lakeland Public Library.*

The businesses have changed, and trees now shade this block of East Main Street, but in 2009 most of the buildings seen in 1924 still exist. The principal exceptions are the addition of the McKay Building at the southeast corner with South Kentucky Avenue and the 1978 loss of the four-story Spencer-Futch Building, which stood on the north side of East Main across from the west end of the Terrace Hotel. *Authors' collection.*

Established in 1890, the State Bank of Fort Meade moved in September 1902 to Lakeland and was renamed the State Bank of Lakeland. In about 1924, Earl Morgan Savage photographed the bank at the southeast corner of East Main Street and South Tennessee Avenue. That year it had assets of $1.8 million, Augustus H. DeVane was chairman of the board and William W. Chase was president. *Courtesy Special Collections, Lakeland Public Library.*

In 1925, offices in the State Bank building were occupied by Bowman Realty Company, physician J.C. Chapman, Orange Belt Realty Company, attorneys H.E. and L.D. Oxford and stenographer Helen Sumner. Tenants in 1936 included realtor J.O. Bloodworth, dentist Robert B. Haddock, physician Andrew J. Harness and George W. Safford. Walgreen Drugs moved into the building in the 1930s. *Authors' collection.*

Mann Patterson Riggins (1827–1895), his brother-in-law Calvin W. Waggoner (1853–1906) and his son Norman Alpheus Riggins (1858–1941) owned the Riggins and Waggoner dry goods store at the southwest corner of East Main Street and South Tennessee Avenue. Their first building is seen here in about 1890, and four of the men on the porch are identified: L.J. Baldrick, Waggoner (third from left), Mann Riggins (fourth from left) and Vick Ellis. *Courtesy Special Collections, Lakeland Public Library.*

By 1909, Norman Riggins had become the sole proprietor of the company—now doing business as "N.A. Riggins"—and had erected a two-story brick building at the same corner. The building was sold after his 1941 death for $85,000. Looking southwest through the intersection, the old Florida National Bank Building (now Wachovia) is visible, as are the Wachovia drive-through in the corner lot, the Colonial Square cupola and a portion of the Polk Theatre at right. *Authors' collection.*

Cadets from the Lodwick School of Aeronautics paraded along East Main Street past the intersection with North Tennessee Avenue during World War II. The school, established by Albert I. Lodwick, provided flight training for over 8,600 British and American cadets between 1941 and 1945. The building to their left is at the northwest corner of the intersection, and with the address of 126–128 East Main Street, it housed the Western Union Company offices. *Courtesy Special Collections, Lakeland Public Library.*

Once known as the Blumberg Building, this structure now exists as the Munn Park Building. Michelle Martin's Main Street Creamery is located at the corner, and the Silver Ring Café faces Munn Park. The next building north, not visible, is the historic Autotel (circa 1927), constructed as a 240-car garage. For nearly twenty-five years it was Morrison's Cafeteria, after the mid-1970s it became Fox 'n Hound clothing store and in 1992 the building was renovated for Citrus and Chemical Bank. *Authors' collection.*

The downtown business district, Munn Park, and the rail yard were thriving in the late 1920s, as seen from the Terrace Hotel. Beautification efforts began in 1888 when the Lakeland Park Association encouraged members to plant a tree or shrub in the park, and enough money was raised to build a pavilion. The traffic signal tower in the intersection of East Main Street and South Kentucky Avenue was constructed in the late 1920s. *Courtesy Special Collections, Lakeland Public Library.*

The appearance of Munn Park has evolved over the decades, even if its general purpose has not. The most dramatic visual change came in the early 1960s, when angular walkways bisected the park and led to a large, irregular "Magic Fountain" that dominated the southern end. Munn Park was redesigned in 1989 to reflect its original "town square era" character and continues to serve as a pleasant public meeting spot anchoring a revitalized downtown business and residential district. *Authors' collection.*

Earl Morgan Savage preserved this view from the Terrace Hotel in about 1925. Looking northwest across Kentucky Avenue toward the railroad station, this perspective offers a look at the top of the Raymondo Block (center foreground), loaded railcars and buildings on East Pine Street north of the station: the Yarnell Building, the extant Union News Company Building (circa 1910) and the Eureka Hotel. *Courtesy Special Collections, Lakeland Public Library.*

More than eight decades have passed since Savage's photograph from the Terrace, and notable changes are evident. The Kress Building displaced most of the Raymondo Block in 1929. Only one railroad track passes through downtown, compared with the thirteen mainline and spur tracks that bisected South Florida Avenue between East Pine and East Main Streets in the mid-1920s. The N. Curtis Peterson state government building has stood since 1984 where freight lines once terminated. *Authors' collection.*

The center of Munn Park is marked by a monument to Confederate war dead dedicated by the Lakeland chapter of the United Daughters of the Confederacy on June 3, 1910, the anniversary of Jefferson Davis's birth. The soldier faces east, and this view looks toward the northwest. The fountain in the foreground of this 1936 photograph is one of several the park has seen, and the railroad station at the north end is a reminder of the part the park played in welcoming visitors. *Courtesy Special Collections, Lakeland Public Library.*

Munn Park is presently surrounded by East Main Street at the south, a parking lot near Cedar Street at the north, North Tennessee Avenue at the west and North Kentucky Avenue at the east. The fountain at the north end of the park was donated by Sarah D. and L. Kirk McKay Jr. and their family. Mrs. McKay, a longtime supporter of the Polk Museum of Art, was the principal donor of the Sarah D. and L. Kirk McKay Jr. Archives Center, which opened in 2009 at Florida Southern College. *Authors' collection.*

Delivery wagons stood at the ready on the east side of the American Railway Express building in 1921, which was located at 101 South (later North) Tennessee Avenue immediately south of the downtown railroad lines. American Railway Express moved goods from railway stations to and from businesses and homes. This Hinkley photograph is one of many local images produced under the imprint of "Hinkley Photo" or "Hinkley-Curtis Photo" in the 1920s. *Courtesy Special Collections, Lakeland Public Library.*

To borrow a phrase, they paved paradise and put up a parking lot. Local delivery needs changed by the 1960s when railroad facilities were removed from downtown, and the American Railway Express building was a casualty from that era. This lot on North Tennessee Avenue is one of many downtown. Unfortunately, the legitimate need for parking here and in other cities has resulted in the irreversible loss of historic structures. *Authors' collection.*

The Atlantic Coast Line Railroad passenger station was situated at the north end of Munn Park in October 1950. This $35,000 station was erected in 1912 as a single-story building but was severely damaged by a February 1918 fire. The brick walls were salvaged and incorporated into a more substantial two-story building, and the station reopened in January 1919. The American Railway Express building is visible beyond the west end of the depot. *Perkins Photographic, courtesy Special Collections, Lakeland Public Library.*

A new passenger train depot opened on September 1, 1961, on the New Tampa Highway, eliminating the need for this station and the surrounding freight facilities. The depot was razed that year and was replaced by a smaller city bus transfer station. Trains still pass through the center of town, but the traffic is greatly reduced compared to decades past. This 2009 photograph shows a freight train passing the former depot site at the Cedar Street parking lot. *Authors' collection.*

In the 1920s, the Jackson and Wilson Hardware shop shared the three-story A.E. Slone Building (1903) on the east side of North Kentucky Avenue with the Hotel Loyal and Café and Central Pharmacy. The hotel, at 203½, advertised clean beds in a fireproof building, and the café sold home-cooked meals for twenty-five cents. Also upstairs was George H. Alfield's Lake Region Land Company. *Courtesy Special Collections, Lakeland Public Library.*

Lofts on the Park is a five-story, $4.5 million, 24,258-square-foot, sixteen-condominium building located at 125 North Kentucky Avenue and the intersection with Cedar Street. Designed by Lunz Prebor Fowler Architects and built by Marcobay Construction in 2006–7, the project was one of several designed to bring residents back to the historic center of town. Another successful effort was Lloyd Boggio's renovation of the New Florida Hotel into seventy-six-unit Lake Mirror Tower completed in 2005. *Authors' collection.*

In 1916, shoppers looking southward along South Kentucky Avenue from East Rose Street saw the Leader dry goods store (102); Henry C. Stevens's jewelry shop, where railroad employees had their watches inspected (104); Roy J. Straw's shoe store (114); and the Welcome Arch. Munn Park is visible on the west side of the street, as is the Deen-Bryant Building facing East Main Street. The Kibler Hotel dominated the skyline past the arch on the east. *Courtesy Special Collections, Lakeland Public Library.*

Munn Park and the Deen-Bryant Building are visible links between 2009 and the previous photograph, as most buildings on the east have been replaced or remodeled. Another structure of note is the Adams Building (circa 1908, as the Bryant Building) at 221 North Kentucky Avenue, behind the viewer's left, site of Traditions Unlimited. The top floors of this three-story rusticated block building were removed, and part of the building was lost when East Pine Street was widened. *Authors' collection.*

A 1936 bicycle parade paused behind a Polk Theatre sedan advertising "Bank Nite" and the murder mystery *Half Angel* starring Brian Donlevy and Frances Dee in front of Montgomery Ward at 117–123 North Kentucky Avenue. Immediately to the south was the Thom McAn shoe store in a remnant of the Raymondo Building (circa 1905), which formerly contained eight stores and forty-eight offices. The southernmost three quarters were removed when the 1929 S.H. Kress and Company Building was constructed. *Courtesy Special Collections, Lakeland Public Library.*

The eighteen-thousand-square-foot Renaissance Revival Kress Building at 109 North Kentucky Avenue was designed by George E. Mackay and L. Seibert. Kress departed in 1975, and the building was renovated in 1982 and 1999. The Kress Building is presently home to the Explorations V Children's Museum, with three floors of hands-on displays of interest to youngsters. Of particular note are the colorful, ornate façade and the twenty-foot-high first-story ceiling. *Authors' collection.*

The Bryant Block is one of the city's oldest, having anchored the northeast corner of East Main Street and North Kentucky Avenue since 1904. The block was constructed by and named for Robert Bryant. In 1924, the J.G. McCrory Company Five and Ten Cent Store was located at the north end, and Malcolm G. Waring's (1886–1964) real estate business was advertised from the second floor, where he had offices for more than twenty years. *Earl Morgan Savage, courtesy Special Collections, Lakeland Public Library.*

In 1980, eighty-three-year-old Olin Bryant, nephew of builder Robert Bryant, recounted, "For us, you had to come downtown to make a day complete. Back then, there were so many people downtown you couldn't walk. It was a madhouse. The people came from all over to shop." The sixteen-thousand-square-foot Bryant Block is presently home to Harry's Seafood Bar and Grill and commercial offices. It was restored in 1988 and purchased in 2005 for $1.4 million by Bryant Block Venture, LLC. *Authors' collection.*

The Munn Building (1904) was located at the southeast corner of East Main Street and South Kentucky Avenue and is most closely associated historically with the First National Bank of Lakeland and its successor institutions. Columbus W. Deen was bank president and J. Wesley Bryant (1845–1926) was vice-president. John L. Fouts purchased controlling interest in 1917, but the bank closed on May 15, 1929. This undated view includes a sign for James R. Boulware's fire insurance agency, with a South Kentucky entrance. *H.A. Kelly, authors' collection.*

Florida National Bank of Lakeland opened on September 13, 1929, but was no longer in the Munn Building when this circa 1952 photograph was taken. The Terrace Hotel was in full operation, as were businesses in the adjacent Drane Building. The Munn Annex (1907) at 108 South Kentucky Avenue displayed a sign for Elmer L. Adams's jewelry store. The Munn Annex was restored in 1987 and was renamed the Munn-Regnvall Building. *Sanborn Photo Service, courtesy Special Collections, Lakeland Public Library.*

The Drane and Munn buildings were demolished to accommodate the 1953 McCrory Company Five and Ten Cent Store, seen here prior to 1980, which in the mid-1960s was managed by James F. Grimsley. After McCrory's closed, the building was vacant for some time before a comprehensive 1985–86 renovation by L. Kirk McKay Jr. The 26,238-square-foot building is now known as the McKay Building. *Courtesy Special Collections, Lakeland Public Library.*

The McKay Building, with a 100 South Kentucky Avenue address, remains an office building, with Merrill Lynch as the principal tenant in space renovated in 2000. Other office suites are occupied by Kelly Services, the Watson Clinic Foundation, the Mims Group, Smith and Thomas Insurance and Reed Appraisal Company. Note the addition of the stair tower on the west side of the Terrace Hotel, added during its 1998 renovation. *Authors' collection.*

Lakeland's Welcome Arch was erected over South Kentucky Avenue about one hundred feet north of East Main Street in 1914 prior to the twenty-fourth reunion of the United Confederate Veterans in November. The monumental sign, illuminated by electric lights and supported by guy-wires to large posts, remained in place for several years. During World War I, it reminded residents to "Be Patriotic, Observe Meatless Tuesdays and Wheatless Thursdays." Signs were occasionally suspended under the arch: "UCV" for the United Confederate Veterans and "CHA" for the Florida Central Highway Association. *Authors' collection.*

Lakeland's whiteway—characterized by streetlights mounted on metal poles at regular intervals along the city's streets—was first illuminated on February 7, 1914. It consisted of sixty-three standards of five lights each, including those along Kentucky Avenue. Nearly one century later, this view along North Kentucky Avenue adjacent to Munn Park hints at a revitalized downtown to be appreciated and enjoyed. Olin Bryant might well approve. *Authors' collection.*

North of Main Street

Florida Avenue delineates the historic separation between west and east Lakeland. In downtown, West Main Street extends west from Florida Avenue, and the same road extending eastward is East Main Street. Until the early 1920s, the north and south dividing point was the Atlantic Coast Line Railroad in downtown, and north and south address numbering commenced there. By 1924 the north–south dividing line was changed to Main Street, and residential and business address numbers were altered to reflect the change. This causes some difficulty in identifying the location of some obscure buildings but aids in dating labeled historic photographs. Throughout this volume, identified street addresses are contemporaneous with the dated image. Additional address information has been provided for buildings constructed before 1924 when the numbering is ambiguous.

The Sanborn Map Company produced hundreds of thousands of large-scale maps illustrating twelve thousand American cities beginning in 1867. The maps were produced for the fire insurance industry and show the location, composition and general function of structures in a community. These maps are an indispensible aid to historical research, and Lakeland Sanborn maps from 1903, 1908, 1913, 1917 and 1922 were consulted for this project.

Another valuable resource for local historians are the old R.L. Polk and Company city directories. The directories list residents with occupation, address and spouse noted; provide a street-by-street listing of residents and businesses; include local demographics and a summary of the locale; and include business advertisements. The Lakeland Public Library maintains an impressive collection of Lakeland city directories.

The images in this chapter are of downtown buildings located on the north side of Main Street and northward, with the exception of Munn Park. The oldest buildings among this group are the most recognizable, including the Bowyer Block (1902) on North Kentucky Avenue, the Clonts Building (1903) on East Pine Street and the Bryant Block (1904) at the corner of East Main Street and North Kentucky Avenue. Each has been modified during generations of use, but all bear resemblance to their original appearance. Another landmark is the old city hall (1913) at the corner of East Main Street and North Florida Avenue, which was substantially altered after government offices moved to a new location.

Hotels and boardinghouses built to support the railroad thrived in this section of downtown during the early 1900s. Among their number were the Glenada Hotel in the Weeks Block on East Pine Street north of the train depot and the two-story Franklin Hotel on North Massachusetts Avenue. Polk County's only cotton gin was located near the Franklin and Lake Mirror, where owner T.L. Hendrix prepared the local crop of Egyptian long-staple cotton for market. Until 1971, an active farmer's market was located downtown behind First Baptist Church. These are all gone and scarcely remembered, but occasional serendipitous discoveries tease one's imagination: renovations in 2005 to the Keller Williams Realty quarters in the 200 block of East Pine Street revealed an original entrance to the Suwanee Hotel. Its connection to Lakeland's past? The top two stories comprised the Glenada Hotel from 1908 through 1916, the Eureka Hotel from 1917 through 1946 and the Park Hotel from 1947 through 1951. Opened in 1952, the Suwanee burned down in March 1968 yet awaited rediscovery.

City marshal Washington H. Tillis escorted Lakeland's first fire truck in a circa 1913–14 parade. The procession is turning onto East Main Street from South (now North) Florida Avenue. Tillis's office was located in the newly constructed city hall building, at the right. The Central Hotel, visible at 102½ South Florida Avenue, was managed by Wright A. Yaun, who resided with his wife, Cora B. Yaun, at 105½ South Florida. *Courtesy Special Collections, Lakeland Public Library.*

North Florida Avenue extends northward from the Main Street intersection toward Lawton Chiles Middle Academy, visible past the railroad crossing signal in 2009. At the northwest corner of this intersection is a portion of 101 West Main (formerly Lakeland Centre), a two-tiered mini-mall of retail and office spaces created from the Oxford block between Missouri and Florida Avenues in 1986–87. The old city hall may be seen at the right. *Authors' collection.*

Lakeland's second city hall was built in 1913 at the northeast corner of East Main Street and South (now North) Florida Avenue, and this postcard image is from that year. The billboard adjacent to city hall promoted the December 4 minstrel and variety show of the Jacksonville-based Rabbit's Foot Company. "The Foots" was organized by Patrick H. Chappelle, was sold to Fred S. Wolcott and starred Ida Cox, Louis Jordan, Gertrude "Ma" Rainey, Bessie Smith and other leading entertainers. *Courtesy Special Collections, Lakeland Public Library.*

After local government offices moved to the new city hall in 1926, it housed various retail establishments. At some juncture, the distinctive tower was removed, but by 1987, local law firm Peterson, Myers, Craig, Crews, Brandon and Mann began to restore the building. Architect John Wallis was presented a unique challenge, as no plans for the tower remained. Using postcards and photographs as a guide, he produced a new tower that is faithful to the original, giving new life to this landmark. *Authors' collection.*

The Hartsell Building (circa 1924) at 106–114 East Main Street was new when Earl Morgan Savage photographed Friendly Drug Store. A second-floor King Insurance Agency sign proclaimed "We Protect You." Architect Edward Columbus Hosford (1883–1939) also designed the 1926–27 Lakeland High School building, and the two structures share some aesthetic similarities. His other work included the stately 1908–9 Polk County Courthouse. He and his wife, Alice Baker Hosford, settled in Lakeland in 1920. *Courtesy Special Collections, Lakeland Public Library.*

Although close to Munn Park, the Hartsell Building likely suffered when retail buildings on the entire south side of the block were demolished in 1973. Exterior alterations covered the transom windows and obscured the first-story exterior brickwork, and the distinctive illuminated awning was removed. Will businesses once again be attracted to this building, as was the Bass-Hamlin Company, which in August and September 1924 advertised "first-class homes, investment property, or insurance" available through its office at 206 Hartsell Building? *Authors' collection.*

Michael F. Hetherington (1867–1938) was a self-made newspaperman who used money earned as a printer's devil to attend college in Kentucky and subsequently purchase the *Lebanon Enterprise*. He moved his family to Miami in 1900 and then to Lakeland in 1904. Here he purchased the *Lakeland News*, and by 1911 it became the daily *Lakeland Evening Telegram*. The Evening Telegram Building constructed in 1913 at 326 East Main Street housed the newspaper and other offices. *Courtesy Special Collections, Lakeland Public Library.*

In 1927, the Star-Telegram Building, as it became known, also housed the Sunday school board of the Methodist Episcopal Church (South), the Polk County Credit Association and the Central Labor Union. By the 1940s, the building had become known as the Florida Citrus Commission Building, and by the 1960s it was the Polk County Administration Building. The building was demolished to make way for the Main Street Parking Garage, completed in 1986. *Authors' collection.*

Access to the railroad was particularly important for Joseph A. Powell's Lakeland Grocery Company, wholesale distributor for his nineteen All American stores. In 1936, this warehouse was located immediately south of the railroad tracks on the east side of North Florida Avenue. The All American stores were purchased by George Jenkins for $175,000 in 1945 and incorporated into the Publix Super Markets chain, which he founded in Winter Haven in 1930. *Dan Sanborn, courtesy Special Collections, Lakeland Public Library.*

This parking lot between North Florida and North Tennessee Avenues south of the railroad track serves customers of BB&T in the Autotel (left) and the old city hall (right), where Ford Heacock's insurance agency is located. Also prominent in this view is the north side of the Hartsell Building (center). The top of the Marble Arcade is visible through the top portion of the railroad signal. *Authors' collection.*

The Academy at the northwest corner of South Tennessee Avenue and East Lime Street was Lakeland's first school. Established in 1884, this gathering spot was where citizens voted to incorporate the city on January 1, 1885. The Lake Wire School (1902) was one of the city's first brick buildings. It became the junior and senior high school and burned down in 1927. This 1927 Lakeland High School building was constructed at the same location. *Courtesy Special Collections, Lakeland Public Library.*

After Lakeland High School departed for a new campus on Bartow Road, Lakeland Junior High School remained in the building, followed eventually by the Polk Opportunity School. Extensive renovation in 1995 preceded the arrival of Lakeland Middle Academy, a magnet school for mathematics, technology and science. The school was renamed Lawton Chiles Middle Academy in 1999 in honor of 1948 Lakeland High School graduate Governor Lawton Mainor Chiles Jr. The building was placed on the National Register of Historic Places in 1993. *Authors' collection.*

L.M. Ballard's *Lakeland News*, the town's first newspaper, was published on June 10, 1884, by Dennis Boully. This two-story newspaper office and general store was located at the northeast corner of North Florida Avenue and East Pine Street. The paper was sold and renamed in 1887, and a successor publication was rechristened the *Lakeland News* by Michael E. Hetherington in 1904. Also visible in this undated photograph are the North Side Hotel, a billiard hall and D.H. Slone's general merchandise store. *Courtesy Special Collections, Lakeland Public Library.*

The wooden sidewalk is long gone. Karl F. Pansler's law firm stands at the corner, and along the shaded street are the Fearn Partnership (106); Landmark Mortgage (110); Rejuvinate Body Works, Satya Life and Vitality Massage (112); Liquid Hair Studio (118); and Edwards Fruit Company, Gulftide Management, Kyra Infotech, Legendary Journeys, Smith Law Group and Wheeler and Wheeler (120). The two-level 284-car parking garage on the south side of the street was completed in the fall of 1987 for $1.3 million. *Authors' collection.*

Works Progress Administration workers in 1938 had the unusual experience of using this privy on East Pine Street upon which a prankster wrote "For Rent." The Yarnall Warehouse and Transfer Company building at 120 East Pine dates from 1920 and was situated close enough to the Atlantic Coastline Railroad freight house, at left, to ensure a steady stream of business. Apartments occupied the second floor; in 1938 there were five occupied apartments and seven vacancies. *Courtesy Special Collections, Lakeland Public Library.*

The Yarnall Building has been occupied almost continuously since 1920. Oscar H. Lewis operated the O.K. Candy Company here in the 1930s and 1940s, and his son Herman owned the successor Mutual Candy and Cigar Company (later Mutual Wholesale) here until 1950. Mathias Raulerson renamed the structure the Raulerson Building in 1952, Alonzo Church Wright opened his Lakeland Federal Savings and Loan in 1962 and Enco Properties sympathetically restored the building in 1990. *Authors' collection.*

In 1942, the Wonder Store was located on the north side of East Pine Street at 220, Jack's Tap Room and Billiards was located at 222, Southern Dime Stores was at 224 and from 1940 to 1947 Lovett's Grocerteria was in the Clonts Building visible to the east. Within several years, Sylvia's Department Store replaced the Wonder Store, and Bob's Trading Place, which featured secondhand clothing, replaced the dime store. *Courtesy Special Collections, Lakeland Public Library.*

In July 2009, this portion of the block included several firms devoted to real estate and related services. Keller Williams Realty was located at 218 East Pine Street; Lake Morton Title, LLC, was at 222 (but by September it was replaced by Florida Family Title); and Keller Williams University was at 224. Only the narrow structure at 224 East Pine bears a resemblance to its 1940s appearance. *Authors' collection.*

Architect Wilbur B. Talley's Clonts Building was constructed for merchant Samuel L.A. Clonts (1856–1925) in 1903 at the northwest corner of East Pine Street and North Kentucky Avenue. This landmark building features distinctive brickwork and Richardsonian Romanesque architectural elements. The Tierra Del Lago Cigar Company produced the popular O-U-No Havana cigar. Clonts and his wife, Hattie, had eight children, and he was Lakeland's mayor in 1898, 1903, 1904 and 1912. *Courtesy Special Collections, Lakeland Public Library.*

Several second-floor windows still advertised "S.L.A. Clonts Real Estate," but the large awning promoted G.P. Murrell's mercantile business: "Murrell and Sharp/Dry Goods, Clothing, Shoes, Notions, Etc./Strictly Cash." The Marcum and Hickson meat market and grocery was next door. Murrell served on the city council and city and county school boards and laid the first brick when the city's streets were paved. *Courtesy Special Collections, Lakeland Public Library.*

The distinctive architecture of the Clonts Building was not entirely diminished by the colorful 1980s painting of Bob's Loan and Sporting Goods, which as "Florida's Most Unusual Store" featured a two-headed calf and displayed weapons dating back four centuries. Established in 1947, from 1976 to 1991 the pawnshop—later an antiques shop—was owned by Frank Ziegele (1941–2001), who was involved with initiatives to restore and beautify downtown. The Landmark Restaurant opened here in April 1994. *Courtesy Special Collections, Lakeland Public Library.*

Since May 2003 Marion Pugh's Patchwork Pig quilting supplies shop has inhabited the prestigious 228 East Pine Street address. The shop features the original fourteen-foot-high tin ceiling, heart pine floors and brick walls. The original pediment facing south was lost during a 1960 tropical storm, and the exterior brickwork remains painted, but the restored Clonts Building remains among Lakeland's most picturesque. *Authors' collection.*

Napoleon B. Bowyer (1832–1910) built the first commercial brick building in 1902 at the northeast corner of North Kentucky Avenue and East Pine Street, replacing D.H. Slone's wooden retail store. The American Red Cross had an office here in 1917, and by the 1950s it housed Polk Paint Company and a grocery. To the north was the Royal Café Building (circa 1913) with a restaurant downstairs and hotel upstairs. *Courtesy Special Collections, Lakeland Public Library.*

The central parapet reading "Bowyer Bldg/1902" is now obscured by lush foliage, and the second-story covered balcony has been removed, but the attractive façade of the Bowyer Building is clearly evident following a 1993 renovation. Brooke Pottery occupies two storefronts in the building and features American fine crafts. The Royal Café Building is now home to Mitch and Michelle Harvey's Mitchell's Coffee Shop, established in 1998. *Authors' collection.*

As early as 1938, the Lakeland Chamber of Commerce was adjacent to Fire Station Number One on the east side of North Massachusetts Avenue, as seen in November 1956. This parcel in the 100 block was also bordered by Cedar Street to the north and by East Main Street to the south and east as it swept around Lake Mirror. The chamber relocated to the Park Trammell Building on Lake Morton in 1966. *Courtesy Special Collections, Lakeland Public Library.*

A modest visual illusion is evident at this spot when one looks from the west side of North Massachusetts Avenue toward the former chamber of commerce site. The space between North Massachusetts and the promenade wall is sufficiently wide to have accommodated East Main Street when it extended behind the chamber, and seventeen-acre Lake Mirror is larger than it appears here. In the distance are the former Coca-Cola bottling plant and Albert Paley's *Tribute to the Spirit of Volunteerism* sculpture, at right. *Authors' collection.*

The Lakeland Police Station and municipal court building was at 125 North Massachusetts Avenue at the southeast corner with Cedar Street. Fire Station Number One, built in 1926 at a cost of $39,625, was south of the police station at 119, and the chamber of commerce was at 115. Police Chief Roy V. Huchingson oversaw the department in 1949 when Duane Perkins photographed these officers and motorized vehicles. *Courtesy Special Collections, Lakeland Public Library.*

The police department moved to new quarters on Lake Wire in 1963, and that building was incorporated into the fire department headquarters. The buildings were demolished in about 1997. In 2007, when East Main Street was rerouted to skirt the north edge of this property, it became part of Allen Kryger Park. The police department moved back to the neighborhood in 1993 to the present station at 219 North Massachusetts. *Authors' collection.*

The Lakeland Terrace Hotel provided the vantage point for this circa 1924 Earl Morgan Savage photograph. Buildings in the center include the two-story Hotel Lakeland on South Massachusetts Avenue and automobile and machine shops facing East Cedar Street. Along the north side of East Cedar were a wholesale grocery, the Lakeland Citrus Company packinghouse, the Lakeland Citrus Growers Association and the Lakeland Light and Water Department plant (1916). The Star-Telegram Building is at bottom left. *Courtesy Special Collections, Lakeland Public Library.*

Lakeland Cash Feed is the only recognizable building in 2009. Beyond Lake Mirror, the Lakeland In-Town Bypass bridge stands over the railroad. The $17.1 million first phase commenced in 2002, and in February 2004 Sebrenia and Jessie McIntyre drove the first car over the bridge. The bypass routes vehicles from Bartow Road to Magnolia Street and then west to North Massachusetts and North Florida Avenues. The second phase to George Jenkins Boulevard was nearing completion in late 2009. *Authors' collection.*

The Lakeland Citrus Growers Association Building (circa 1924) was at 510 East Cedar Street, formerly part of East Rose. The association represented the marketing and general farm business interests of growers. This building was on the former site of the Lakeland Feed and Supply building adjacent to the Lakeland Light and Water Department. In 1928, the department was managed by Charles Larsen, the lighting capacity was nine thousand kilowatts and the water system had a daily capacity of six million gallons. *Courtesy Special Collections, Lakeland Public Library.*

Lakeland Cash Feed, established by William Leon Jackson in 1918, moved into the building in 1930 and has been a fixture ever since. "Where nutrition comes first" was more than just a motto; until 1962 the company specialized in vitaminization in on-site manufacturing of livestock and poultry feed, including Lakeland College, Bingo, Imperial and Jacko feeds. The current address is 502 Lake Mirror Drive, and the closest neighbor to the east is the Amtrak Train Station. *Authors' collection.*

The Lakeland Ice and Fuel Company wagon made regular deliveries from 1102 North Omohundro Avenue. Located at the northwest corner with Second Street northwest of downtown, the company was one block east of the Federal Ice and Refrigerating Company, a major producer with railroad access. Eddie Hagen and William A. Damon are shown in 1927 or 1928 as they deliver ice on North Iowa Avenue near the East Oak Street intersection. The company was owned by O. Garnett Stone and advertised coal, coke, wood and ice deliveries. *Authors' collection.*

The Parker Street neighborhood was bisected by Lakeland In-Town Bypass construction in 2002. By mid-2007, the Lakeland Downtown Development Agency (LDDA) and the city had purchased 59 properties east of North Massachusetts Avenue and north of the railroad line to the bypass. The site was designed to accommodate 449 townhomes and condominiums, and Feltrim Development was selected as developer in 2006. At the time of this writing, the old structures are gone, but the economic recession has delayed construction. *Authors' collection.*

This A&P Super Market branch store was located at 820 North Massachusetts Avenue from about 1942 to 1950. Another branch of the Great Atlantic and Pacific Tea Company, as A&P was known formally, was located at 301 South Florida Avenue. In 1936, the building (then numbered 818–820) was shared between the Montgomery Ward and Company warehouse in the south end and Florida Palm Furniture Company in the north. *Courtesy Special Collections, Lakeland Public Library.*

The Check-R-Board Feed Company and H&H Storage were located in this building in 1952, Imperial Polk Feed and Farm Supply was here in 1957 and in 1965 the Mather of Lakeland Furniture dealers made use of the spacious facility. At some juncture the parapet was removed. The old A&P is now empty, with "no trespassing" signs posted along the front façade. *Authors' collection.*

John Franklin Cox (1874–1924) moved to Lakeland in 1890 and developed a successful real estate business. Active in civic affairs, he served as mayor from 1905 to 1907 and again in 1911, 1916 and 1917. The John F. Cox Grammar School was constructed in 1928 at the northeast corner of East Memorial and Lakeland Hills Boulevards, where the latter is a practical continuation of North Massachusetts Avenue, and functioned as a school until 1990. *Dan Sanborn, 1937, courtesy Special Collections, Lakeland Public Library.*

Known before its closing as the John F. Cox Elementary School, the building was placed on the National Register of Historic Places in 1999. In 2001, the Watson Clinic Foundation purchased the land and building from the city and the Polk County School Board for one dollar and renovated it for use by Lakeland Volunteers in Medicine as "a volunteer-run medical clinic that provides free quality medical care to the working uninsured of Polk County." The former school is now known as the Hilda Sutton and William D. Blanton Building. *Authors' collection.*

Lakeland's most distinctive landmark was envisioned by chamber of commerce manager Tom Appleyard in the early 1920s. The Lake Mirror Promenade and Civic Center (1928) was designed by prominent civil engineer Charles Wellford Leavitt Jr. (1871–1928), leader of the "City Beautiful" architectural movement. It includes a 6,900-foot concrete seawall around much of Lake Mirror, a 540-foot concrete retaining wall, Corinthian columns and grand staircases descending from Allen Kryger Park around a vaulted loggia. *Courtesy Special Collections, Lakeland Public Library.*

Leavitt's project included a bandstand on the southeast shore of the lake near shuffleboard courts and lawn bowling greens. The deteriorating condition of Lake Mirror Promenade inspired Mildred Grizzard and Jean Bunch to form Historic Lakeland, Inc., in 1979, and the organization's visionary efforts led to the $750,000 Promenade restoration, completed between 1983 and 1987. Lake Mirror Park and a new amphitheatre were dedicated in 1999, and showpiece Hollis Garden opened on the southeast shore in 2000. *Authors' collection.*

South of Main Street

In the early 1900s, downtown from Main Street south four blocks to Lake Morton included a concentration of businesses close to Munn Park and residences to the south. While hotels and boardinghouses closer to the railroad offered temporary housing, the neighborhood approaching Lake Morton was full of stately family homes. This pattern eventually changed as commercial buildings spread southward, where railroad traffic and the extensive network of downtown rail lines could be avoided.

One grouping of attractive residences was located close to the present city hall. The homes belonged to Morris G. and Anna Belle Munn (412 East Orange Street), Christopher Gustavus and Mary Lee King Memminger (417 East Orange), J.D. and Alice A. O'Hearn (401 South Massachusetts Avenue) and Henry B. and Lula S. Carter (501 South Massachusetts). The Carter home was later relocated to south Lakeland, where eventually it became the home of country music stars George Jones and Tammy Wynette. The Munn and Memminger homesites were cleared for construction of the Florida Citrus Mutual headquarters.

The Chautauqua Movement that had originated in New York State in the 1870s provided entertainment and educational programs throughout America until the 1920s. The programs became popular in Lakeland thanks to the efforts of C. Rucker Adams, and a local Chautauqua auditorium was constructed at the eastern terminus of Main Street on Massachusetts Avenue in 1912. Among the distinguished guest speakers was "the Great Commoner," populist William Jennings Bryan. The distinctive venue was removed when the Lake Mirror Promenade and Civic Center project was constructed.

Lakeland's first school is also long gone. The wood-frame Academy constructed in 1884 for $300 also hosted public and religious gatherings before local congregations were firmly established, and several churches were organized at the school. The Academy was replaced in 1902 by a brick schoolhouse located between North Florida Avenue and Lake Wire Drive. Nearly 160 former students gathered for a 1959 reunion marking the seventy-fifth anniversary of the school's opening, and a plaque was placed on the then new General Telephone (now Verizon) building marking the location of the school.

This chapter includes images of downtown in the general area bounded by South Florida and South Iowa Avenues and by East Main Street and Lake Morton. Among the notable buildings in this section are the Lakeland Terrace Hotel (1924, also known as the Hotel Lakeland Terrace), Polk Theatre (1928), the Marble Arcade (1926), the Oates Building (1925), the New Florida Hotel (1926–35, now Lake Mirror Tower) and the Park Trammell Building (1927). Interestingly, these were all products of the Florida land boom, during which time Lakeland saw steady growth in population, industry and tourism, and these buildings are all still in use.

The Herron Building was located at 115–119 East Main Street, facing north. In 1936, from east to west, the storefront was shared by Miss Manona Herron's millinery shop and her brother Reuben R. Herron's clock shop (119); Stephens's Grocery, an affiliate of the Independent Grocers Alliance (IGA, at 117); and the Kirby Music Company (successor to Yates Music House, at 115). *Courtesy Special Collections, Lakeland Public Library.*

Known variously as "Herron's Opera House" and "Herron's Theatre," the second story of the Herron Building opened in October 1908 as an entertainment and meeting center and was where the Lakeland Board of Trade was organized in 1911. By 1936, the opera house had been converted to general office space. The building was replaced by the J.C. Penney Company store, which moved to spacious new quarters in 1973, and the entire block of buildings was razed that year. *Authors' collection.*

Abraham G. Munn built the three-story Tremont House (later Hotel) in 1885 with an expansive lawn overlooking Lake Mirror, and it developed a reputation as one of the finest in south Florida. The hotel was moved to 113 South Massachusetts Avenue in 1923 to make way for the $750,000 Lakeland Terrace Hotel, seen during construction in early 1924. The Terrace opened in October 1924 to great fanfare and replicated the Tremont's fine reputation. The Tremont Hotel was demolished in 1936. *Earl Morgan Savage, courtesy Special Collections, Lakeland Public Library.*

The Lakeland Terrace remained the city's premier hotel until the 1970s, when altered traffic patterns and the proliferation of hotels away from downtown exacted a slow decline. The building was closed in 1986 and faced an uncertain fate. Rob Scharar purchased the property in the mid-1990s and poured $7 million into an inspirational sympathetic renovation. The hotel reopened on February 26, 1999, and has reclaimed its title as Lakeland's most elegant hostelry. *Authors' collection.*

Herbert Jackson Drane (1863–1947) constructed his handsome Drane Building (1909, 1911) on the south side of East Main Street between South Kentucky and South Massachusetts Avenues. This Sanborn Photo Service image likely dates from the 1940s, when George L. Gaines Jeweler and the Juvenile Ship were located within. A Railway Express Agency truck was parked in the adjacent alley. Terrace Drugs was located in the east end for many years. *Courtesy Special Collections, Lakeland Public Library.*

This 2009 view of the McKay Building was taken from the site of the four-story Spencer-Futch Building at 318 East Main Street. Real estate developer Lawrence M. Futch established the Futch Undertaking Company in 1910, and Edwin Spencer Jr. was a local attorney. In the 1930s and 1940s, the building was known as the Citrus Commission Building, and from the 1950s until its 1978 demolition, it was known as the Professional Building. The Marble Arcade is visible in the distance. *Authors' collection.*

Cumberland Presbyterian Church was organized in 1888, and its first home was this wooden frame sanctuary at the northeast corner of South Florida Avenue and East Lemon Street. The building was constructed in 1905 at a cost of $2,000 on a lot donated by Frances Jane Cherry Riggins, widow of Mann Patterson Riggins. The congregation relocated in 1925 to a new home at 730 South Florida Avenue, on land donated by Norman and Sallie Riggins. *Courtesy Special Collections, Lakeland Public Library.*

Colonial Square was constructed in the early 1960s at 124 South Florida Avenue, an address formerly associated with Dutch Kitchen Restaurant. The building was treated to a $2.1 million renovation by owners Brian and Sidney Philpot in 2001, in part encouraged by a series of similar projects that saw nine downtown office buildings remodeled in 2000 and 2001. In 2009, the building is home to Regions Bank, Philpot Law Group, Buckner Commercial Properties and Land One Company. *Authors' collection.*

The panoramic photographs extending across these pages chronicle dramatic change looking north through the intersection of South Kentucky Avenue and East Lemon Street. This image, taken after 1919 and before 1924, shows Helen Cochrane's popular boardinghouse, which stood at the present location of the Marble Arcade. "Miss Helen" was active in civic affairs and owned several downtown properties. *Courtesy Special Collections, Lakeland Public Library.*

The west side of South Kentucky Avenue in this block features good food, general merchandise and professional services: Mid-Florida Federal Credit Union (129), Raymond James Financial Services (129), Mitchell's (129), Good Buddies BBQ (127), the General Store (125; say hello to Sparky), Fast Frame (117), Pipo's Cafe (115) and Molly McHugh's Irish Pub (111). Longtime Lakelanders remember this block as the site of Henley's Drug Store (123), Snyder's Shoe Store (117, complete with a merry-go-round) and Myrick's Men's Store (113). *Authors' collection.*

The Hotel Thelma stood vigil over this corner for nearly fifty years. Among businesses located in the hotel were Frank McKay's furniture company in 1914, Haskell Development in 1927 and Armstrong's Grill in 1950. Visible at the north end of the block are the Munn Building and Annex and the Casino Theatre, predecessor to Henry B. Carter's Palace Theatre. The Casino façade had a rounded parapet, and the large sign seen here faced Munn Park. *Courtesy Special Collections, Lakeland Public Library.*

The Hotel Thelma was replaced by a single-level string of commercial spaces in what is now the Carr Building. The Lakeland Terrace Hotel may be seen in the center distance. Businesses along the east side of South Kentucky Avenue include Fresco's Bakery and Bistro (132), Scrapbook Street (128), the Chop Shop (126), the Gym Sports Bar and Grill (118), Palace Pizza (114), Hurricane Alley (112) and Wallis Murphey Boyington Architects (110). *Authors' collection.*

This 1939 photograph shows the restaurant and Federation Natural Food Center at 312–314 East Lemon Street, which were behind the Thelma Hotel. The building served a number of purposes over many years; in 1925 it was Ruby Daniels's newsstand and bookstore, by the late 1930s it was an antique store and in 1950 it was the Model Book Shop. The New Florida Hotel is visible to the east across South Massachusetts Avenue. *Courtesy Special Collections, Lakeland Public Library.*

Looking northeast across East Lemon Street affords a clear view of one of the parking lots now used by Lakeland Terrace Hotel guests and businesses in the Marble Arcade. Across South Massachusetts Avenue stands the parking deck constructed on the north side of Lake Mirror Tower when it was renovated in 2005. On the horizon is the Lakeland In-Town Bypass bridge near Lake Mirror. *Authors' collection.*

The Paul B. Bellew real estate offices were located at 127 South Massachusetts Avenue across from the New Florida Hotel in October 1952. Bellew specialized in appraisals and home, grove and industrial property sales. The home previously was owned by the Louis W. Cowdery family. Cowdery (1856–1916) moved to Lakeland in 1884 and with F.L. Brooks established a general merchandise business. He developed substantial holdings along what was known as Cowdery Block. *Courtesy Special Collections, Lakeland Public Library.*

Seen from All Saints' Episcopal Church, this view through the intersection of South Massachusetts Avenue and East Lemon Street shows the rear of the Carr Building, old Palace Theatre and the Munn-Regnvall Building. The Lakeland Terrace Hotel is at right. The south side of East Lemon was transformed in 1992 by the pedestrian-friendly Lemon Street Promenade, which is between South Florida and South Massachusetts Avenues and now features sculptures from the Florida Outdoor Sculpture Competition. *Authors' collection.*

This westward view from the New Florida Hotel in 1955 captured a busy downtown. Notable landmarks along South Kentucky Avenue were Bible Presbyterian Church (215), Kirk McKay, Inc. (205), Maas Brothers (202), Schwobilt Clothes (201), Hotel Thelma (132–136) and the Marble Arcade (131). On South Tennessee Avenue were the Gilbert-Washburn Hotel (221), Daugherty Building (211–213), Albritton's Women's Shop (119) and Florida National Bank (113–115). *Courtesy Special Collections, Lakeland Public Library.*

This perspective from the ninth floor of Lake Mirror Tower (the former New Florida Hotel) reveals how the downtown landscape has changed. Businesses facing East Lemon Street are gone, the Carr Building occupies the Hotel Thelma site and Colonial Square rises above South Florida Avenue. Of particular note at left is the 63,675-square-foot, $10 million SunTrust Plaza (1999) at 210 South Florida, the first office building constructed in central downtown since 1986. The Lakeland In-Town Bypass bridge near Kathleen Road is visible on the horizon at right. *Authors' collection.*

Grace Lutheran Church was organized in 1908 and 1909 largely through the efforts of Valentine Van Huss, and ground was broken for a sanctuary in 1911. The church was located at the southeast corner of South Tennessee Avenue and East Orange Street. In 1955, the property was sold for $75,000 to First Federal Savings and Loan Association, and the church relocated to 745 South Ingraham Avenue. *Courtesy Special Collections, Lakeland Public Library.*

Offices for Wachovia Bank are now located at the Grace Lutheran Church site. Lakeland had nearly twenty organized churches by the 1920s, many located in or near downtown. Among those not mentioned elsewhere herein were the First Baptist Church on North Florida Avenue, First Presbyterian on South Massachusetts Avenue, Foster Memorial African Methodist Episcopal on West Orange Street, Mount Pleasant African Methodist Episcopal on South Ohio Avenue, Wesley Memorial Methodist Church on North Massachusetts and Zion Hill Primitive Baptist on West Lime Street. *Authors' collection.*

Mabel C. Morrow rented furnished rooms from the 1930s through 1950s at 417 East Orange Street in the Palms, former home of Christopher Gustavus and Mary Lee King Memminger. Mining engineer Memminger helped develop the phosphate industry in Polk County and became a mine manager of considerable influence, also serving as president of the State Bank of Lakeland and on the Lakeland City Council. *Courtesy Special Collections, Lakeland Public Library.*

The Christina phosphate mining community south of Lakeland was named for the Memminger's only daughter, Christine Gustava Memminger. Their home was named for the many varieties of palms planted there and was featured on early postcards of fine residences. The Florida Citrus Mutual Building was constructed on this block in 1951. The Citrus Mutual has been dedicated since 1948 "to helping Florida citrus growers produce and market their crops at a profit" and is the state's largest cooperative grower organization. *Authors' collection.*

The Southern Printing Company at 209 East Lime Street was also promoted as the "Florida Methodist Publishing Company" and the "Office of the Florida Christian Advocate." Guy Hawkins Wilson came to Lakeland in 1923 as manager of this general commercial printing firm, a post he held for a number of years. Wilson's father was Methodist minister J. Edgar Wilson, longtime editor of the *Florida Christian Advocate*. By 1950, this building housed the McDaniel Printing Company. *Courtesy Florida United Methodist Conference Archives.*

A parking lot now occupies the Southern Printing Company site in this view toward the southeast. The general dentistry practice of Dr. Siuhung Fan is located at 211 East Lime Street (left). The frame building beyond the light post is the carefully restored offices of Hauger-Bunch, Inc., Realtors at 415 South Kentucky Avenue. This is one of the last remaining grand residences in the downtown district, owned in the 1940s and 1950s by Hal and Gladys Register; Clare and Sallie Lou Henley lived next door at 421. *Authors' collection.*

Earl Morgan Savage captured this busy scene in about 1925 looking southwest along South Florida Avenue from city hall at the East Main Street intersection. The Polk County Trust Company building at 101 was constructed in 1912 as the Hardin Building. Dentist D.M. Sears was at 107½ above the Zig Zag Grocery, and Robert Duff's Hardware shop was in the W. Fisk Johnson Building. South Florida Bus Service number eight approaches on the left; company offices were at 110 East Main. *Courtesy Special Collections, Lakeland Public Library.*

Peoples Savings Bank opened in the Polk County Trust Company building in 1931, remaining until a 1964 move to South Missouri Avenue. Founded by C.F. Smith and C.V. McClurg, the McClurg family retained control of Peoples Bank until it merged with Huntington Bank in 1996. The building known since 1984 as the C.V. McClurg Building acquired an Art Deco styling in 1942 and a new brick exterior in 1983. Now it is home to the Bank of Central Florida, founded in March 2007. *Authors' collection.*

In the 1950s, the W. Fisk Johnson Building (1912) at 113–115 South Florida Avenue was the site of the Lakeland Business Institute, established in 1927; Western Union, advertising Easter telegrams; and Todd Hardware. Wilbur Fisk Johnson's real estate business had been located in the Raymondo Building on the east side of Munn Park in 1913; that year he and Nora K. Johnson made their home at 805 South Florida Avenue. *Courtesy Special Collections, Lakeland Public Library.*

The W. Fisk Johnson Building has served general retail and commercial purposes in recent years. Continental Travels was in the building when in 1983 it became the first downtown building placed on the state of Florida's list of certified historical buildings, restored to its original appearance. When the adjacent building to the north was demolished, a painted sign reading "Willard Battery Service Station" was exposed. *Authors' collection.*

Pilots in training from the Lodwick School of Aeronautics traveled to the Polk Theatre to watch Tyrone Power and Betty Grable in their 1941 film *A Yank in the RAF.* James Melton launched construction of the theatre in 1926 but exhausted his capital soon thereafter. The unfinished theatre was sold to Paramount's Publix theatre chain, and on December 22, 1928, the movie *On Trial* was the first shown. The house had one thousand seats downstairs and seven hundred in the balcony, and three movies were shown each week. *Courtesy Special Collections, Lakeland Public Library.*

This beautiful, atmospheric theatre features twinkling stars on a cloud-covered ceiling, a terrazzo floor and an interior reminiscent of a Renaissance Italian courtyard and villa. The theatre hosted many live performances, including appearances by Tom Mix, Tommy and Eddie Dorsey, Eddie Duchin, Elvis Presley and Sally Rand. The theatre was saved from demolition by Polk County Landmarks, Inc., in 1984. It was painstakingly restored and represents a place of pride for Lakelanders who attend events in this remarkable venue. *Authors' collection.*

The Lakeland Bottling Works was located on the east side of South Florida Avenue in the 200 (now 100) block from 1907 to 1912. In 1913, the business was at 408 North Vermont Avenue, with William L. Smith as proprietor. By 1925, the Coca-Cola plant was bottling eight thousand bottles daily under the direction of Dickson F. Jackson for customers in Lakeland, Mulberry, Auburndale and Polk City. In 1931, the Lakeland Coca-Cola Bottling Company was located at 115 South Lincoln Avenue. *Courtesy Special Collections, Lakeland Public Library.*

In 2009, the Ledger Building—long since converted to other uses—is where Lakeland Bottling Works once stood. This block was particularly active during the 1940s and 1950s. A stroll down the east side of South Florida Avenue in 1947 found Nelson's Jeweler (106), Cleghorn's Barber Shop (108), Seminole Café (110), the Ledger Building (112–114), Kirby Music Company (116), Sherrill's Gift Shop (118), Florida Furniture Company (120), Dutch Kitchen (124) and Davis Pharmacy (126). *Authors' collection.*

Newspaperman Samuel Howard Farabee (1882–1939) arrived from North Carolina in 1924 and in September of that year established the *Lakeland Evening Ledger*. Michael E. Hetherington, who until 1920 owned the *Lakeland-Star Telegram*, wrote in 1928 that "Mr. Farabee's editorials, always temperate, sane, and constructive, have been a definite force for all that is good and progressive." This photograph depicts the Ledger Building at 112–114 South Florida Avenue. *Courtesy Special Collections, Lakeland Public Library.*

The *Lakeland Evening Ledger* and *Lakeland-Star Telegram* merged in July 1927, and the *Ledger* has been published continuously since that time. The old Ledger Building still stands on South Florida Avenue, having been used most recently as a bank office with two drive-through entrances on the north façade leading to a single exit on South Florida. The *Ledger* presently occupies a $72 million facility completed in 1998 at 300 West Lime Street. *Authors' collection.*

In 1924, F. Mortimer Pratt operated a garage at 114 South Florida Avenue adjacent to the Ledger Building in this view northward along that thoroughfare. Several automotive sales and service outfits existed close to the city's center. The Lakeland Automobile and Supply Company north of Main Street was an agent for Hupmobile, Ford and Cadillac in 1916. Also that year, Abbott Detroit Sales Company sold and serviced Hercules and Abbott automobiles. *Courtesy Special Collections, Lakeland Public Library.*

This photograph looking north on South Florida Avenue was taken from between Polk Theatre and the Colonial Square office building. Visible on the west side are the W. Fisk Johnson Building, C.V. McClurg Building, West Main Street, 101 West Main, the railroad line, the Lakeland Bus Terminal and Lawton Chiles Middle Academy. On the east side are the old Ledger Building, East Main Street, old city hall and, beyond the railroad, Trinity Presbyterian Church (formerly First Baptist). *Authors' collection.*

In 1952, the Lakeland Home Appliance Company, managed by Howard H. Enlow, was located at 226–228 South Florida Avenue in a building immediately adjacent and attached to the extant Oates Building. The Mediterranean Revival–style Oates Building was constructed in 1925 and was home to the Oates Corley Furniture Company (later the Oates Furniture Company) until 1967. The building was placed on the National Register of Historic Places in 1995. *Courtesy Special Collections, Lakeland Public Library.*

A service wing added by Jerry Herring in 1994 for the Oates Building exists where the Lakeland Home Appliance Company once stood. Herring carried out a sympathetic restoration of this Lakeland landmark, including an addition of a new floor between the third and fourth levels made possible in the original building plans. Offices of the State of Florida Department of Tax Revenue, the General Tax Administration and Child Support Enforcement are now here. *Authors' collection.*

This distinctive home at 115 (formerly 211) South Tennessee Avenue was owned by William E. and Dorothy J. Browning. A home here in 1903 may have been remodeled before 1908 to become this home. Also at this address as late as 1924 was Annie Browning, who in 1910 unveiled the new monument to Confederate war dead in Munn Park. In 1925, the residence contained offices for architect A.E. Scotini, and in 1938 the City Hat Shop was here. *Courtesy Special Collections, Lakeland Public Library.*

The Browning residence was demolished in about 1940 to make way for the Florida National Bank Building (1942) at 113 South Tennessee Avenue. Following a 2002 merger, the Art Deco building has operated as a branch of Wachovia. This architectural jewel features a high coffered ceiling and cast-iron teller cages. A curious feature is observable on the north and south façades: the north finish is complete but the south is not, due in part to the proximity of a once-adjacent neighbor. *Authors' collection.*

The Daugherty Building was constructed on the west side of the 100 block (later the 200 block) of South Tennessee Avenue in about 1922. Architect Wilbur B. Talley had an early office here and was joined in 1924 by the Walton School of Commerce and Finance. In 1955, the Polk Federal Savings and Loan at 213 South Tennessee and Arthur H. Miller's Hardware and Paint Company at 211 were the principal tenants. The building was demolished in 1996. *Courtesy Special Collections, Lakeland Public Library.*

By the 1970s, the southernmost storefronts included only single doorways, and the distinctive transoms along the entire building were covered. Last known as the Daugherty-Fenton Building, the edifice was traded by Attorneys' Title Service to the Lakeland Downtown Development Authority (LDDA) in 1982 or 1983 in exchange for a building at 121–123 North Kentucky Avenue. James H. Edwards of the LDDA noted in 1996 that "the plan of the second floor…was an 'H' [design] so that windows could be provided to interior offices." *Authors' collection.*

The Washburn Hotel was constructed by William Daugherty for Harry D. Washburn at 221 South Tennessee Avenue in 1923 at a cost of $125,000. By the time of this December 1948 photograph, the establishment had been renamed the Gilbert-Washburn Hotel, which included the Gilbert Coffee Shop. New owner Arthur Gilbert also owned the Gilbert Motor Company at 420 West Main Street, which sold and serviced Studebakers. *Courtesy Special Collections, Lakeland Public Library.*

Seven buildings on the block bounded by South Tennessee and South Kentucky Avenues, and East Lemon and East Orange Streets were demolished by Eagle Amalgamated of Gibsonton in 1996. The seventy-three-year-old Gilbert-Washburn hotel and all of the buildings in its block also fell, except for the Oates Furniture Building, then occupied by the *Tampa Tribune*. The SunTrust Building (1999) may be seen beyond the 288-car three-level parking garage. *Authors' collection.*

Fresh-cut flowers lined the entry of Reed's Flower Shop at 231 South Tennessee Avenue in April 1938. The shop was owned and operated by Josephine Reed and her son and daughter-in-law, Foster B. and Nettie Reed. Their van stood poised to deliver FTD orders with the speed of Mercury to lucky customers throughout Lakeland. Across East Orange Street stood the four-story 1926 Peninsular Telephone Company building at 301–303 South Tennessee Avenue. *Dan Sanborn, courtesy Special Collections, Lakeland Public Library.*

The imposing Peninsular Telephone Company building was home in the 1930s to Fancy Fare Restaurant, the Florida Inspection and Rating Bureau, the Lakeland Highlands Cooperative Association and various insurance agencies. Peninsular Telephone moved here from offices in the Kentucky Building. In 2009, the Verizon building at the northwest corner of South Tennessee Avenue and East Lime Street peeks past the corner of the parking garage where Reed's Flower Shop once stood. *Authors' collection.*

Walgreen Drugs replaced the familiar State Bank of Lakeland corner clock with its own sign when it opened here in the 1930s. This view of Walgreen along the east side of South Tennessee Avenue dates from April 1951, when the building included offices for dentist R.B. Haddock, realtors and insurance agents Fusselle and Hook and the Sanborn Camera Centre. Owner Harold Sanborn, his brother Dan and Duane Perkins were instrumental in chronicling mid-century Lakeland. *Dan Sanborn, courtesy Special Collections, Lakeland Public Library.*

In recent years, the former bank and drugstore building at 201 East Main Street was home to Antiques on Main Furniture. NuJak Development renovated the exterior in 2004 and completed a $200,000 office space renovation in 2005 preceding occupancy by WellCare of Florida insurance agency. Frank Kendrick established NuJak in 1992, and joined by Tim Jackson and Lee Brunson, the firm specializes in construction, property development and commercial real estate services. *Authors' collection.*

The 98,080-square-foot Vanity Fair Arcade at 114–116 South Tennessee Avenue has a central hallway providing access to shops within the building, much like a modern shopping mall. This photograph by Earl Morgan Savage dates from about 1924 and shows the west façade. Savage's shop and photography studio were located in the arcade, and as he was only in Lakeland for two or three years, his photographs provide an examination of a precisely identifiable period in the city's history. *Courtesy Special Collections, Lakeland Public Library.*

The Vanity Fair Arcade was remodeled with an unfortunate Art Deco–like styling in the 1940s, but a $440,000 renovation completed in 2002 by Andy Norman brought back the luster of the original design. The Mark Twain Smoke Shop, now at 124 West Main Street, was the Vanity Fair Arcade's signature retail occupant for years. In 2009, businesses include Tropical Smoothie (116, #101), Meyer Law Group (116, #115) and DMA Engineering (116, #201). *Authors' collection.*

The year 1918 brought the completion of a $75,000 United States Post Office building at the northeast corner of South Tennessee Avenue and East Lemon Street. This March 2, 1918 image of the southeast corner and east façade was submitted by the building superintendent as evidence of the current state of construction. James A. Wetmore was acting supervising architect, and the contractor was Wise Granite and Construction Company of Richmond, Virginia. *Authors' collection.*

This was Lakeland's first purpose-built post office building. Earlier facilities were located in commercial office buildings bordering Munn Park, often as a lure to shoppers. An addition to the north end was constructed in about 1924 and the east wing is not original. The building became known as the Federal Building and provided space for Internal Revenue Service offices and recruiting stations for the U.S. Navy, U.S. Marine Corps and U.S. Army. The building is presently vacant and faces an uncertain fate. *Authors' collection.*

Sixteen-year-old Priscilla Eveleth of Winter Haven was the national baton-twirling champion in 1936 and led that year's Lakeland Armistice Day parade past the Palace Theatre on South Kentucky Avenue. That same year Eveleth was awarded Winter Haven's Banker's Cup for meritorious community service and received a Distinguished Service Medal awarded by the 1936 Cleveland Great Lakes Centennial Exposition. *Courtesy Special Collections, Lakeland Public Library.*

When the Casino Theatre opened in 1913 at 114 South Kentucky Avenue, it was one of Lakeland's first full-size motion picture houses. It was rebuilt by prolific Jacksonville theatre architect Roy A. Benjamin (1888–1963) as the 1,551-seat single-screen Palace Theatre in 1925. The Palace served for several decades but was closed by the 1960s. The theatre was renovated for office and retail space in 1997, and for many, the only clue to the building's past is the name of Patricia Schiano's Palace Pizza restaurant. *Authors' collection.*

Lakeland's first large, modern hotel was constructed in 1913 by brothers Adolphus B. and David B. Kibler at the northeast corner of South Kentucky Avenue and East Lemon Street. The $125,000 Kibler Hotel was sold for $200,000 in 1919 to Henry B. Carter (1872–1924), who renamed it Hotel Thelma in honor of his daughter. A 1924 advertisement promoted the 120-room, 80-bath hotel as "the Highest Point in South Florida." *Courtesy Special Collections, Lakeland Public Library.*

Hotelier Henry B. Carter arranged for construction of the Palace Theatre adjoining Hotel Thelma shortly before his untimely death in an automobile accident. The hotel's distinguished guests included Theodore Roosevelt, Henry Ford, Roy Rogers, Louis Armstrong, Thomas Edison and many Florida governors. Unfortunately, the Thelma suffered a loss of profitability in the 1950s, and the site of important civic and social functions for nearly half a century was demolished in May 1962. *Authors' collection.*

Lakeland's first high-rise was the ten-story Marble Arcade at 129 South Kentucky designed by Roy A. Benjamin, completed in 1926. Heating and plumbing systems were installed by the firm of Joseph E.H. Dorsett of Lakeland. The W.P. McDonald Company occupied nine office suites when the building opened. The firm was owned by William P. McDonald of Lakeland and Flushing, New York, an influential road contractor and one of the city's first millionaires. *Hinkley-Curtis, 1925, courtesy Special Collections, Lakeland Public Library.*

The 40,530-square-foot Marble Arcade was remodeled in 1959 during a brief period when it was known as the Broderick Building, a certified historic renovation was completed in 1988 by Folsom Construction and NuJak Construction completed an exterior renovation in 2003. MidFlorida Federal Credit Union CEO Kevin Jones reported in 2006 that its headquarters moved downtown because the area held promise: "When we moved in, several of the buildings were vacant. [This area] really has become the jewel of Lakeland." *Authors' collection.*

The First Methodist Episcopal Church (South) sanctuary and parsonage were located at 303–305 (later renumbered 215) South Kentucky Avenue from 1906 to 1951. The distinctive castle-like appearance of the "gray stone church" was enhanced by the rusticated block exterior. Reverend J. Milburn McLeod oversaw a move to a new site on the east side of Lake Morton, and the downtown site was purchased by Bible Presbyterian Church. *Courtesy Florida United Methodist Conference Archives.*

Bible Presbyterian Church was organized by members of First Presbyterian Church in November 1950, and the former First Methodist Church site was purchased for $100,000 in 1951. In 1961, it became Kentucky Avenue Presbyterian Church, and in 1969 it was renamed Covenant Presbyterian. The congregation relocated that year, and the Kentucky Avenue site was razed. The three-story, thirty-eight-thousand-square-foot Heritage Plaza was completed in November 2001 on East Lemon Street. *Authors' collection.*

The cornerstone for the $75,000 Lakeland Elks Club building at 108 South Massachusetts Avenue was laid on March 29, 1917. Subsequently greatly expanded, the building served as the Hotel Elk with a full-service restaurant. The building to the north was the Chautauqua Auditorium (1912), demolished in 1925 when the Lake Mirror Civic Center project commenced. The building was vacated in 1984 and demolished in 1991. Lakeland Lodge number 1291 BPOE is now at 4529 Harden Boulevard. *Hinkley Studio, authors' collection.*

Allen Kryger Park was dedicated in November 2006 in memory of the Lakeland businessman and philanthropist, who died in 2002. Funded by Lynn Fischer-Kryger, Robert Kryger and the city, the spacious open park on the west side of Lake Mirror overlooks the Frances Langford Promenade, which in March 1946 was dedicated in honor of *Time* magazine's "Sweetheart of World War II," who grew up in Lakeland. Langford's signature tune was "I'm in the Mood for Love." *Authors' collection.*

The Florida Hotel was constructed in 1926 at 128–130 South Massachusetts Avenue. Then unfinished, the hotel opened in September 1926 but fell victim to the Florida land bust and the Great Depression. The Order of Railway Conductors opened and completed the rechristened New Florida Hotel in 1935. In 1938, the Business and Professional Women's Club was located here, as were the ninth-floor offices of the Lake Region Broadcasting Company and realtor Willard V. Hallam. *Sanborn Photo Service, courtesy Special Collections, Lakeland Public Library.*

The New Florida Hotel was converted to an independent senior living center in 1962 and in 1980 was renamed Regency Tower. The building fell into disrepair after closing in 1996 and was threatened with demolition to make way for a formal garden. Among the ideas proposed to save the structure was reuse as the law school for Florida A&M University. The hotel was thoroughly renovated and reopened in 2005 with luxurious living spaces as Lake Mirror Tower. *Authors' collection.*

Clinton V. McClurg's Lakeland Guest House was at 227 South Massachusetts Avenue in August 1952. A sign for optometrist Richard Ryer was in the front corner window. This view from city hall toward the northwest shows a portion of the Hotel Thelma on South Kentucky Avenue. A Maas Brothers department store opened at the north end of this block on November 1, 1954. *Courtesy Special Collections, Lakeland Public Library.*

The 1954 Maas Brothers department store was demolished after this 140,000-square-foot two-story building was completed in 1970. Maas Brothers and J.C. Penney, which relocated nearby in January 1973, were both connected to the Lakeland Parking Garage. Maas Brothers was consolidated with Burdines, and Burdines and J.C. Penney left downtown for new homes in Lakeland Square Mall. This building was remodeled for Watkins Motor Lines in 1995, which was purchased by FedEx in 2006. *Authors' collection.*

Lakeland's present city hall, seen here in 1940, was constructed in 1926 on the site of an orange grove donated by Morris G. Munn, who moved to Lakeland in 1901 and became associated with his father Abraham G. Munn's Lakeland Improvement Company. The 1,500-seat City Auditorium (1926), later renamed the Harry S. Mayhall Auditorium, was located between city hall and All Saints' Episcopal Church (1923). *Sanborn Photo Service, courtesy Special Collections, Lakeland Public Library.*

Mayhall Auditorium as a cultural center hosted hundreds of events, including the 1950 Florida Federation of Music Clubs convention, graduation ceremonies for Florida Southern College and performances by the Lakeland Little Theatre and the Lakeland Symphony Orchestra. Deemed too expensive to renovate, the sturdy auditorium was razed in 1969. The auditorium lot was used for parking until a forty-thousand-square-foot architecturally compatible city hall addition was completed in 1991. *Authors' collection.*

This Mediterranean Revival–style Public Library was constructed in 1927 at the base of South Massachusetts Avenue with the address 35 Lake Morton Drive. Lakeland civic buildings constructed along Massachusetts as part of a $9 million program inaugurated during the mayoral term of John W. Buchanan Jr. included Fire Station Number One, the City Auditorium (1926), city hall (1926) and the library. The latter three were designed by Franklin O. Adams Jr. *Dan Sanborn, 1938, courtesy Special Collections, Lakeland Public Library.*

The Public Library building was renamed in 1955 for Lakeland native Park Trammell (1876–1936), mayor from 1899 to 1903, a state representative and senator, state attorney general from 1908 to 1913 and Florida's twenty-first governor from 1913 to 1917. Trammell was a U.S. senator from 1917 to 1936. The Lakeland Public Library moved to 100 Lake Morton Drive in 1966, at which time the Greater Lakeland Chamber of Commerce moved to the Park Trammell Building, where it remains. *Authors' collection.*

Around Town

Lakeland is quite naturally known for its beautiful lakes; today, the city of Lakeland contains thirty-eight named lakes and numerous smaller bodies of water composing approximately 45,000 acres. The smallest is 2.5-acre Lake Blanton, and the largest is Lake Parker, at 2,272 acres. Lake Mirror, Lake Wire and Lake Morton are closest to downtown, and each has been affected by its proximity to growth. The city's Lakes Program has worked since 1988 to improve the quality of the lake and water resources. Major projects have included the dredging of approximately three million cubic yards of sediment from Lake Hollingsworth and ongoing plant management. This commitment to restoration and management assures that these community assets will remain healthy and attractive.

The Charles Leavitt–designed Lake Mirror Promenade and Civic Center affected the shape and function of Lake Mirror. A clear source of civic pride, the Promenade gained broader attention when illustrated in the January 1930 issue of *National Geographic* with the caption, "Like the ornate entrance to some vast Venetian palace looms the Civic Center of Lakeland." Continuing, the photograph description read, "Rising on Mirror Lake like a fairy city on an iridescent sea, Lakeland, for its size, presents one of the most charming appearances of any city in the South." Leavitt developed the entire south shore as a pedestrian-friendly park and warned that the city should refrain from routing automobile traffic through this area. It took twenty-five years, but the state did extend East Lemon Street around the lake in 1953, which both reduced the aesthetic appeal of the Promenade and caused damage to the structure.

Unfortunately, time was not kind to the Lake Mirror Promenade, and by the late 1970s it was in desperate need of repair and renovation. Enter Historic Lakeland. This grass-roots organization worked to increase public concern over the condition of the Promenade, and the site was added to the National Register of Historic Places in 1983. Over a four-year period it was restored using generous donations, federal grants and city appropriations, and it was rededicated on July 3, 1987. The Lemon Street extension was closed in 1998, Lake Mirror Park and a new amphitheatre were dedicated in 1999 and Hollis Garden was completed in 2000, restoring the aesthetic heart of Lakeland. The work of Historic Lakeland has continued with great effect.

The images in this chapter are from the vicinity of Lake Mirror, Lake Morton and South Florida Avenue in the Dixieland Historic District. These neighborhoods were settled soon after Lakeland's founding and include examples of evolving residential, civic and commercial architecture. A small number of photographs of historic structures from outlying areas are also included.

Important aspects of Lakeland's development and history remain and deserve to be told. Your story will add to the collective legacy that Lakeland's citizens leave for those who follow. Share what you know with others, consider what impact our actions have for the future and support local organizations dedicated to preserving Lakeland's unique history.

Physician William Rowan Groover lived on Lake Morton Drive for more than thirty years after his 1898 arrival. He was president of the Southern Finance Corporation and owned five area groves, including one on the shores of this picturesque lake. During the 1920s, the Lakeland Sanitarium owned by Dr. M. Grace Blackman Hanna was located on Lake Morton Drive. The sanitarium had previously been located downtown in the State Bank of Lakeland building. *Courtesy Special Collections, Lakeland Public Library.*

Lakeland is famous for its swans. A pair purchased in the mid-1920s lived on Lake Bonny and precipitated creation of the city's Swan Department. U.S. Air Force sergeant Robert Pickhardt was instrumental in securing the famous donation of two royal swans from Queen Elizabeth of England in 1957, and today there are approximately two hundred swans divided between several lakes. Much of the care they receive has been courtesy of veterinarian Wade G. Gardner and his practice. *Authors' collection.*

Ledger photographer Wilson M. "Hap" Harper photographed the Lakeland Public Library at its new location on the east side of Lake Morton at East Palmetto Street. The library opened in May 1966 on the former site of the Lake Morton School (1914), which burned down on February 21, 1963. The school was the city's main elementary school until several new grammar schools opened in the mid-1920s. *Courtesy Special Collections, Lakeland Public Library.*

The 1966 library was designed by Jones Renfroe Setliff and built by the P.J. Callahan Company. The lakeside circular drive was removed during the 1983–85 expansion, and renovation was designed by Michael B. Furr of Straughn Furr Associates. Today's Lakeland Public Library has two additional locations: the Larry R. Jackson Branch Library at 1700 North Florida Avenue and eLibrary South Lakeland, which opened in July 2007. *Authors' collection.*

The Lake Morton Apartments were constructed in 1948 by Grover J. Carter of Orlando. Located at 175 Lake Morton Drive, the complex featured seventy-two residential units: sixty-eight four-room and four three-room. The apartments were purchased by Florida Southern College in 1954 and 1955. The college sold the property in 1962 for $415,000 to Atlanta-based Allied Associates Investment Corporation. This photograph dates from about 1948. *Courtesy Special Collections, Lakeland Public Library.*

The city's Lake to Lake Bikeway encircles Lakes Hollingsworth, Hunter, Wire and Morton and parallels roadways between these lakes and elsewhere. Residents of Lake Morton Apartments are situated near the center of the bikeway, and their proximity to downtown is enviable. Historic structures on Lake Morton Drive include the Sorosis Club and Woman's Club buildings, both constructed in 1928; the clubs merged in 1986 to become the United Women's Club of Lakeland. *Authors' collection.*

Earl Morgan Savage recorded this circa 1924 view of the traveling Grocerteria wagon in front of the picturesque Wilsonian Apartments. The Mediterranean Revival sixteen-unit apartment building was built in about 1920 at 183–185 Lake Morton Drive and is visible on several period postcards. The Grocerteria—a self-service grocery store—was located in the Adams Building (circa 1908) on North Kentucky Avenue. Many of Lakeland's seventeen thousand residents then lived close to downtown. *Courtesy Special Collections, Lakeland Public Library.*

Within view of the Wilsonian Apartments, where Lake Morton Drive meets Success Avenue, stands one of the city's monumental oaks. It was reportedly spared by Mann Riggins when he cleared land for a citrus grove in the 1880s. In 1897, John F. Cox proposed to his wife under the tree, and when his Dixieland neighborhood grew up around the tree, he made certain that new Success Avenue avoided the oak. Both tales are likely true. *Authors' collection.*

The Colonial Apartments building was constructed in 1913 at 41 Lake Morton Drive by Lakeland pioneer Spence Minor Stephens (1862–1925). Architect Wilbur B. Talley designed the $15,000 edifice in a Neoclassical Revival style. Known later as Freeman Apartments, then a Florida Southern College dormitory and fraternity house, the building was Lakeshore Hotel from 1948 to 1975. *Wilson M. "Hap" Harper, courtesy Special Collections, Lakeland Public Library.*

Need warehouse space? Call the Ruthvens. Local businessman Joe P. Ruthven purchased the Lakeshore Hotel in 1975 and renovated the striking building for office space. Ruthven served as mayor in 1971, and his model of public service—and that of his brother-in-law, Florida governor Lawton M. Chiles—likely prompted his daughter Kay Ruthven Hagen's successful 2008 campaign to become a U.S. senator from North Carolina. *Authors' collection.*

Mosswood has overlooked Lake Morton since 1904, when it was constructed for Norman and Sallie Riggins and their family. The property included a boathouse, gardens and a tennis court, the remnant of which was evident in March 1950. In October 1952, the home was moved across South Tennessee Avenue from 169 Lake Morton Drive and stands at 121 Mosswood Road. After surviving division into apartments, Mosswood has been restored to its former grandeur. *Courtesy Special Collections, Lakeland Public Library.*

The former Mosswood home site is now the Lake Morton Community Church property. The church is affiliated with the Evangelical Free Church of America, and Pastor Tom LaVallee has led the congregation for more than a dozen years. The worship center at left was completed by Rodda Construction in 2005. Also in the neighborhood is First United Methodist Church, located at 72 Lake Morton Drive. *Authors' collection.*

This undated Union Metal promotional photograph shows lighting standards the company installed around Lake Mirror in 1927 and affords a panoramic view from the east shore. Downtown landmarks include the New Florida Hotel, Hotel Thelma, Marble Arcade, First Presbyterian Church, Tremont Hotel, Hotel Elk, Terrace Hotel, Star-Telegram Building and the fire and police stations. Views like this were used in local company advertisements. *Courtesy Special Collections, Lakeland Public Library.*

Charles Leavitt's Lake Mirror Promenade and Civic Center design called for installation of a large ornamental monument on the east side of the lake. It was not until April 2004 that his plan was realized with installation of Albert Paley's thirty-five-foot sculpture *Tribute to the Spirit of Volunteerism.* Paley was selected by a local steering committee formed at the suggestion of Polk Museum of Art director Daniel Stetson. *Authors' collection.*

Lakeland's first electric plant was privately owned and was located at the corner of East Cedar Street and South (later North) Massachusetts Avenue. In 1891, Lakeland joined Tampa and Jacksonville as Florida's only cities with electricity. The city purchased the plant in 1904 and in 1916 constructed a replacement plant on the north shore of Lake Mirror. The plant was gradually enlarged and remained until the McIntosh Power Plant opened on Lake Parker in the early 1970s. *Courtesy Special Collections, Lakeland Public Library.*

The Amtrak Train Station now occupies the Lake Mirror power plant site. The station was dedicated in February 1998 and passenger traffic has returned to the downtown area. The station, now bordered by an extension of the Lake Mirror Promenade, was designed by Wallis Murphey Boyington Architects and built by Marcobay Construction. Amtrak's Silver Star passenger train passes through town twice daily on the New York–Miami route. *Authors' collection.*

The Coca-Cola Building (1936) on the east shore of Lake Mirror was photographed by Art Smith in 1948. When constructed, the $30,000 plant was capable of bottling up to ninety bottles per minute. The façade is embellished with relief panels adorned with the scripted Coca-Cola logo and bottles. The bottling plant closed in 1972. *Courtesy Special Collections, Lakeland Public Library.*

The fire station on North Massachusetts Avenue was seventy years old in the mid-1990s, and the city and department considered various options for a new central station and administrative office. Juanita Black, past president of Historic Lakeland, argued in 1995 for incorporating the Coca-Cola plant into a new fire complex. The additional cost was eventually deemed acceptable, and in 1997 the new facilities opened, wrapped in an irreplaceable historic exterior. *Authors' collection.*

Tourist clubs were formed in Florida cities to enhance winter tourism and promote local growth. The Lakeland Tourist Club was established in 1922, and the city maintained a twelve-acre camp with amenities available free of charge to tourists. The $40,000 Lakeland Community Center (1938) at 760 East Orange Street was also known as the Tourist Club building, and many club dances, teas and various other activities were held here. *Sanborn Photo Service, courtesy Special Collections, Lakeland Public Library.*

By the early 1960s, the Lakeland Community Center was referred to as the Magnolia Building and continued to host meetings and special events. The Garden Bistro restaurant opened in part of the facility in September 2003. The adjacent Hollis Garden (2000) was named for Mark and Lynn Hollis, major contributors of the transformative 1.2-acre botanical garden. The garden has water features and thousands of plants and has become a favorite wedding venue. *Authors' collection.*

To the east of the Magnolia Building were shuffleboard courts and three lawn bowling greens, which saw heaviest use during the winter. These were removed after a replacement lawn bowling green opened in November 2003 at the Thomas R. Shaw Complex in Lake Parker Park. The state-of-the-art artificial green is home to the Lakeland Lawn Bowling Club. Adjacent facilities support the Lakeland Shuffleboard Club. *Courtesy Special Collections, Lakeland Public Library.*

The three-acre Barnett Family Park and the Peggy Brown Building both opened in December 2004. The park was a gift from Carol Jenkins Barnett and Barney Barnett. With a "zero depth" interactive water fountain, a play area, a labyrinth and a large open space, it offers something for everyone. Named in honor of former mayor Winifred "Peggy" Brown, the two-story building offers shaded seating for park-goers and banquet, dance and meeting space. *Authors' collection.*

Working specifications for the Police and Court Building at 20 Lake Wire Drive, "dedicated to better law enforcement," were completed in December 1961, and it was constructed and equipped in 1962 and 1963 at a cost of $570,000. The building was designed by Thomas V. Talley (1904–1975), son of architect Wilbur B. Talley, and was built by the Hodes and Cumming Construction Company. *Courtesy Special Collections, Lakeland Public Library.*

The police station was vacated in 1993 when the Lakeland Police Department moved to a new headquarters building at 219 North Massachusetts Avenue, and it was renovated for commercial office space. The building presently is home to the advertising sales force of Bright House Networks; the ASC Geosciences engineering firm; and Gevity, a human resources support company. *Authors' collection.*

Cumberland Presbyterian Church (1925) at 730 South Florida Avenue was designed by Herbert D. Mendenhall, also the architect of All Saints' Episcopal Church on South Massachusetts Avenue. Mendenhall platted the Dixieland, Shore Acres and Casa Bella subdivisions, and in 1925 he employed thirty-four engineers and over one hundred engineering assistants locally. This Dan Sanborn photograph dates from April 1961; the minister was E. Crawford Williams. *Courtesy Special Collections, Lakeland Public Library.*

Calvin and Margaret Waggoner arrived in Lakeland in 1884 and built a two-story home—complete with a wind-powered well—in what is now the 200 block of South Tennessee Avenue. The home was carefully dismantled after 1906 and reassembled on Riggins Street, where it served as a manse for Cumberland Presbyterian Church when the church was constructed. The church was renamed Westminster Presbyterian Church in 1942. *Authors' collection.*

The Ducky-Wucky Restaurant at 940 South Florida Avenue was a drive-through with curb service in 1934 when purchased by husband and wife Reece and Clifford Stidham. They combined their first names to rechristen the establishment Reececliff, and a Dixieland institution was born. Reececliff was operated by Mrs. Stidham and their daughter, Mildred Stidham Pope, and the restaurant remained in their extended family for many years. *Courtesy Colby Brown and Cissy Brown.*

The drive-through was enclosed in 1947 by Mildred Stidham and Charley Pope, and the entire restaurant was extensively remodeled and enlarged in 1992. Bob Pope Sr. and Bob Pope Jr. were instrumental in the restaurant's success, the latter becoming owner in 1982; and Jeanette Mobley, Jo Young and Adena Reynolds have been long-tenured employees. Today Reececliff is owned by restaurateur James Bronkhorst, who has also owned the Lakeland eatery Harry's at 1003 East Main Street and the Harbor Side Restaurant in Winter Haven. *Authors' collection.*

This 1951 photograph depicts the Frostproof High School marching band parading north through Dixieland on South Florida Avenue between Charles and Patterson Streets. On the east side were Gable's Radio, Record and Appliance advertising Kelvinator products (1042 South Florida); McCoy's Metal Shop (1046); Fenton's Laundry (1048); and the Radio Accessories Company (1050). *Courtesy Special Collections, Lakeland Public Library.*

This stretch of Dixieland on South Florida Avenue offers retail and professional services. Among the businesses are Walt Witte and Sons (1026), Laser Recharge (1030), Joyful Heart FHC (1032), Clipper Ship Barber Shop (1035), Swilley Curtis Mundy Hunnicutt Associates Architects (1036), Art in Motion Academy of Dance (1037), Bomar Trophy Shop (1051) and Bent's Schwinn Cyclery (1058 and 1066). The Dixieland Post Office has been located at 1047 South Florida since the 1940s. *Authors' collection.*

That Dixieland was a de facto extension of downtown is amply illustrated in Arthur Perkins's July 1957 view northward along South Florida Avenue from the corner of Patterson Street. The crowded business district included Myrt and Mary's Gift Shop (1049), Lakeland Home Freezer Center (1045), Dixieland Pharmacy (1043), South Florida Variety Store (1041), chiropractor William H. Miller (1037), Strickland's Upholstering (1035), Acme Jalousie Company (1027) and Raymond Ziegele's Dairy Queen (1008). *Courtesy Special Collections, Lakeland Public Library.*

Businesses still line South Florida Avenue in Dixieland, but the density of retail establishments in this section has diminished. The Bomar Trophy Shop has been here for years, as has Dean and Kay Shimer's local favorite Subs 'n Such restaurant in the old Dairy Queen. The area is encompassed by the City of Lakeland's Dixieland Community Redevelopment Area, described as "a vibrant commercial district that is home to a variety of local businesses and a number of historic commercial structures." *Authors' collection.*

This distinctive building at 1101 South Florida Avenue was the site of Pipkin's Ice Cream Parlor in 1947, owned by Reuben O. Pipkin. His Pipkin Dairy operated for nearly seventy years until September 1991, when it was sold by his son Curtis Pipkin. By 1954, this building had become Pipkin's Dixieland Maid Rite, in 1963 it was Koin Kleen Laundry and Hungry Howie's Pizza arrived in 1988. *Courtesy Special Collections, Lakeland Public Library.*

Dixieland near Park Street, like the 1000 block, is lined with restaurants, retail and similar businesses. Among those to the north are consulting firm Black Cypress, Emerald Commercial Funding and attorney Edward A. Jacobson (1102), as well as Framing Master, Sylvia's Salon, architects Melton and Associates and Modular Plans Design Company (1074). To the south are Swift's Shoe Repair (1115), Lakeland Lock and Safe (1117), Grass Root Organic Restaurant (1212), Miss Carla's (Betsye Kay's) School of Dance (1214) and Hattie's Branches (1224). *Authors' collection.*

A large crowd turned out to hear evangelist Lloyd King speak at Southside Baptist Church in 1937. The church was organized by Pastor P.C. Barkley in 1922, and this handsomely appointed sanctuary stood at the northeast corner of McDonald Street and Pennsylvania Avenue from 1924 until 1979. A new sanctuary was dedicated in 1967, and education buildings were erected in 1948 and 1981. The property was sold in 2008, and the congregation relocated to the Florida Baptist Children's Homes chapel. *Dan Sanborn, courtesy Special Collections, Lakeland Public Library.*

St. Joseph's School was established in 1938 on Missouri Street adjoining St. Joseph's Catholic Church at 210 West Lemon Street. In 2008, the Diocese of Orlando purchased the four-and-a-half-acre former Southside Baptist Church campus and extensively renovated the buildings in preparation for the 2009–2010 school year. Approximately 170 students in preschool through eighth grades enjoy the sixty-six-thousand-square-foot facilities. Monsignor John P. Caulfield is pastor and Lana Swartzwelder is the principal. *Authors' collection.*

The largest single-site concentration of architect Frank Lloyd Wright's structures is his "Child of the Sun" campus at Florida Southern College. Wright designed eighteen structures for the school, and twelve were constructed between 1938 and 1958. The most widely recognized is Annie Pfeiffer Chapel (1941), built at a cost of $100,000. The exterior walls are made of approximately six thousand tapestry blocks in forty-six different designs. This photograph dates from after 1944. *Courtesy Florida Southern College Archives.*

This view of Annie Pfeiffer Chapel shows the northeast corner of the building. The Esplanade leading to the left was reconfigured when the Polk County Science Building was constructed in the late 1950s. Responsibility for preserving Wright's work has been enthusiastically embraced by college president Anne B. Kerr. The college received a Campus Heritage Grant from the J. Paul Getty Foundation in 2006 to develop a plan for long-term stewardship of the campus. *Authors' collection.*

The sweeping steps and plaza between Annie Pfeiffer Chapel and Wright's E.T. Roux Library provided the setting for a group of art students painting campus scenes in the 1950s. Restoration architect Jeff Baker of Mesick-Cohen-Wilson-Baker Architects of Albany, New York, has led work on the Water Dome (1948) and Annie Pfeiffer Chapel. The World Monument Fund named the "Child of the Sun" campus to its 2008 World Watch List of the one hundred most endangered sites in the world. *Courtesy Florida Southern College Archives.*

By 2009, this view was largely unchanged, except for the removal of dormer windows from Joseph-Reynolds Hall (1922) beyond the Esplanade. The Florida Southern College buildings were recognized in Frank Lloyd Wright: From Within Outward at the Guggenheim Museum, an exhibit marking the fiftieth anniversary of Wright's death. President Kerr hosted the gala event "An Evening at the Guggenheim" for two hundred friends and alumni of the college during the exhibit. *Authors' collection.*

Roux Library at Florida Southern College was the backdrop for Kathy Jo Clark, Marilyn Clayton, Brenda Davis and Kathy Jones, seated at the edge of the J. Edgar Wall Plaza in September 1968. The four Lakeland High School seniors were on campus for a *Highlander* photo shoot. The library was completed that fall and replaced the E.T. Roux Library (1945) designed by Frank Lloyd Wright. *Perkins Photographic, courtesy Special Collections, Lakeland Public Library.*

The Wall Plaza was originally designed by Frank Lloyd Wright as the Water Dome, with water cannons at the perimeter to send water cascading toward the middle of a 160-foot pool. Only the pool was constructed during 1947 and 1948 at a cost of $15,000, and it was partially filled when Roux Library was built. A restoration was completed in 2007, and today this remarkable structure demonstrates the college's commitment to Wright's cherished legacy. *Authors' collection.*

Located west southwest of downtown, Central Avenue Grammar School at 604 South Central Avenue was constructed in 1926. The architects were Poteet and Whitworth, who also designed the John F. Cox Grammar School on North Massachusetts Avenue. This 1938 Dan Sanborn photograph shows the front of the school, facing north along West Hickory Street. Joyce Davis noted in *Lakeland's Unique Architectural Heritage* that by 1985 the ends of the school were sinking. *Courtesy Special Collections, Lakeland Public Library.*

The school became known as Central Avenue Elementary School and was added to the National Register of Historic Places in 1999. The elementary curriculum was discontinued in 1991, and the building is now the West Area Adult School. Administrator Loretta B. Cameron oversees a series of free and moderately priced programs for adults who did not finish high school. Among the selection are reading, writing and mathematics classes, as well as instruction in computers, family literacy and English for Speakers of Other Languages (ESOL). *Authors' collection.*

The red brick Dixieland Grammar School was built at a cost of $67,500 in 1924 during a momentous wave of civic infrastructure expansion. The property at 416 Ariana Street was purchased from realtor William Leffie Thompson for $12,500, and the school enrolled neighborhood students, many of whom previously attended the Lake Morton School. This 1938 Dan Sanborn photograph shows the original building prior to addition of a west wing. *Courtesy Special Collections, Lakeland Public Library.*

Dixieland Elementary School is led by principal Debbie Henderson, and the expanded building continues to serve the Dixieland Historic District. The school underwent a $1.5 million renovation in 1993, and in 2009 food service manager Cindy Wickham was honored as the Polk County School Board's school-related employee of the year. Ten-acre Dobbins Park west of the school received a $340,000 upgrade in 1997 and now has a half-mile walking path, pavilions, athletic courts and other amenities. *Authors' collection.*

Dan Sanborn captured this view of Cleveland Court Elementary School at 328 East Edgewood Drive in 1938. The school was opened in 1927, but shrinking enrollment coupled with the Florida land bust caused its closure after less than one year. The school was used as a vocational school and as a Work Projects Administration (WPA) facility during World War II. The school reopened in 1947 and has served as a school ever since. *Courtesy Special Collections, Lakeland Public Library.*

Cleveland Court marked its fiftieth anniversary in 1997, and leading to that observance it created a courtyard with commemorative bricks honoring students, teachers, friends and alumni. The grounds were recently enhanced by a bird habitat created by Eagle Scout Johnny Jackson from Boy Scout Troop 760. Daniel Lunn has served as the principal of Cleveland Court Elementary School since 1998. The school was placed on the National Register of Historic Places in 1999. *Authors' collection.*

The Lakeland Municipal Airport was established on the west shore of Lake Parker in 1935. This group of air school students was photographed in about 1936; instructor Walter Haldeman is at the right. The air school was one of a number of Works Progress Administration projects that benefited Lakeland's citizenry. The Works Progress Administration was renamed the Work Projects Administration in 1939. *Courtesy Special Collections, Lakeland Public Library.*

The municipal airport was used during World War II as a training ground for British and American pilots. After the Lodwick School of Aeronautics closed, the airport was used by Albert Lodwick to repurpose military aircraft for civilian use. Renamed Al Lodwick Field in 1948, the airport served for another decade before Drane Field in southwest Lakeland became the municipal airport. The remaining hangars are adjacent to Joker Marchant Stadium and exist as part of Tigertown. *Authors' collection.*

Dedicated in 1928, the sprawling 1,700-acre Carpenters Home complex was a retirement community for qualifying members of the United Brotherhood of Carpenters and Joiners of America; this photograph was taken as construction was underway. Residents of the complex received food, clothing, medical care and access to recreational facilities. By 1949, superintendent Marshall Goddard had been associated with the Carpenters Home for twenty years. *Courtesy Special Collections, Lakeland Public Library.*

The Carpenters Home closed in the 1970s, and part of the site was purchased by the Carpenter's Home Church in 1979. A megachurch opened west of the historic Carpenters complex in 1985, and a new retirement home was constructed between the two buildings. For years the church's Evangel Christian School held classes at the complex. Following the 2005 sale of Carpenter's Home Church to Without Walls International Church, and the school's closing the following May, the Carpenters Home has been silent. *Authors' collection.*

Bibliography

City of Lakeland Community Development Department. *A Walking Tour of Downtown Lakeland*. Brochure. Lakeland, FL: City of Lakeland Community Development Department, 2007.

Davis, Joyce M. *Lakeland's Unique Architectural Heritage.* Lakeland, FL: Polk Museum of Art, 1987.

Dunn, Hampton. *Yesterday's Lakeland.* N.p., 1976.

———. *Lakeland, A Pictorial History: A Revised Edition of Yesterday's Lakeland.* Norfolk/Virginia Beach, VA: Donning Co., 1990.

Flekke, Mary M., and Randall M. MacDonald. *Lakeland.* Postcard History Series. Charleston, SC: Arcadia Publishing, 2005.

Haggard, Theodore M. *Florida Southern College, Lakeland Florida: The First 100 Years, An Illustrated History, 1985.* Lakeland, FL: Florida Southern College Press, 1985.

Hetherington, M[ichael] F. *History of Polk County, Florida: Narrative and Biographical.* Saint Augustine, FL: Record Company, 1928.

Homan, Lynn M., and Thomas Reilly. *Lakeland*. Images of America Series. Charleston, SC: Arcadia Publishing, 2001.

Junior Welfare League of Greater Lakeland, Inc. *This Was Yesterday: A History of Lakeland, Florida*. [Lakeland, FL]: Junior Welfare League of Greater Lakeland, Inc., 1973.

Lakeland City and Polk County Directories, R.L. Polk and Company, various years.

[Lakeland] *Ledger*, various dates.

Lakeland, Polk County, Florida. Maps. New York: Sanborn Map Company, 1903, 1908, 1913, 1917, 1922.

The Lake Mirror Story: 1924–2009. Written by Jean Bunch. DVD. Lakeland, FL: Historic Lakeland, Inc., 2009.

MacDonald, Randall M., Nora E. Galbraith and James G. Rogers Jr. *The Buildings of Frank Lloyd Wright at Florida Southern College*. Images of America Series. Charleston, SC: Arcadia Publishing, 2007.

Pinkston, Margaret D[arracott]. *Mosswood Remembered*. Baltimore, MD: Gateway Press, 1995.

Sage-Gagne, Waneta. *Pilots in the Sun: Primary Pilot Training Schools in Lakeland and Avon Park, Florida, 1940–1945*. Lakeland, FL: Friends of the [Lakeland Public] Library, 1990.

Sawyer, Martha. "Polk's Past." *Ledger*, various dates.

About the Authors

Randall M. MacDonald is the director of Roux Library at Florida Southern College. He has been at the college since 1986, following experience in public librarianship and records management. His undergraduate degree was in history, and his graduate work was in library science and education. His previous books include *The Internet and the School Library Media Specialist: Transforming Traditional Services* (1997) and *Successful Keyword Searching: Initiating Research on Popular Topics Using Electronic Databases* (2001, with Susan Priest MacDonald). He has coauthored four previous local history titles: *Lakeland* (2005, with Mary M. Flekke), *Cypress Gardens* (2006, with Mary M. Flekke and Sarah E. MacDonald), *The Buildings of Frank Lloyd Wright at Florida Southern College* (2007, with Nora Galbraith and James G. Rogers Jr.) and *Sebring* (2008, with Susan Priest MacDonald and the Sebring Historical Society).

Susan Priest MacDonald is a fifth-generation Floridian and Lakeland native. She received bachelor's and master's degrees in library science from Florida State University. She is a school librarian and has worked for the School Board of Polk County for twenty-three years, the past eleven at Lawton Chiles Middle Academy. This is the third book she has coauthored, following *Successful Keyword Searching: Initiating Research on Popular Topics Using Electronic Databases* and *Sebring*.

Sarah E. MacDonald is a Lakeland native and student of art history and architecture. She is a graduate of Asheville School in Asheville, North Carolina, and Florida Southern College. One of her goals is to hike to the tallest point in each state. She previously coauthored *Cypress Gardens*. IWGBTP.